THE DRAMA OF SALVATION

THE
DRAMA
OF
SALVATION

Rosemary Haughton

A CROSSROAD BOOK
The Seabury Press   New York

The Seabury Press
815 Second Avenue
New York, N.Y.   10017

Copyright © 1975 by The Seabury Press, Inc.
Designed by Paula Wiener
Printed in the United States of America

LIBRARY OF CONGRESS CATALOGING IN PUBLICATION DATA

Haughton, Rosemary, 1927–
    The drama of salvation.

    "A Crossroad book."
    1. Religious drama—History and criticism.
2. Salvation in literature. I. Title.
PN1880.H35   809.2′51   75-14301
ISBN 0-8164-1201-4

Contents

Introduction

THE purpose of this short book is to clarify a complex and controversial subject by trying to rediscover its dynamics from within. In this way it may be possible to see that apparently irreconcilable notions of what happens under the heading of "salvation" are, in fact, evidence of a polarity that is essential to the thing itself. The chief means used here to explore the human experience of God's saving action is the study of drama. I hope the reason for the suitability of this, at first sight, idiosyncratic exercise will become apparent. But it is worthwhile, even at this stage, to give some explanation for what may seem an arbitrary choice.

The reason is—and this must be taken on faith for the moment—that the dynamics of the drama are not merely an image of the way salvation works, which is a fairly familiar notion, but, more importantly, are an example of the way in which the spiritual energy—the stuff of salvation—has to work, according to its own inherent nature, as something happening in, to, and between people. Dramatic presentation is only one of the many ways this power is developed, but it is one in which that use is necessarily most deliberate and has the widest range of both opportunities and difficulties.

The other arts can, perhaps, help us to see just where they can offer us less—or more. The visual arts depend on the power moving in the artist, but, while the picture or statue may result from a disciplined outbreak of "inner life," the spectator does not see this happen, but only sees the results. The communication may be just as powerful but it is indirect, which may be why some contemporary artists have tried to break down this time-barrier by very direct "action" techniques or by using moving parts. The particular kind of discipline of a musical performance, while it involves (in live performance) a direct communication, also requires that the player or players "disappear" in the music; their service as intermediary between composer and listener is spoiled if their own visible personality obtrudes. Personal interpretation and spiritual power is vital, but the visual element is minimal. Performers who have aggressive personal mannerisms or who wear eye-catching clothes do not enhance their musical reputation, though they may attract attention.

Literature, in book form, can be the most powerful and intimate communication of all: the author's own inner life has unlimited freedom to play on the imaginative powers of the reader, unhampered by any restriction other than that of those same powers. But the communication is one-to-one, no matter how many copies are published. Reading a book is not normally a communal experience, so the element of community-making, which is obvious in the effect of great music or drama on an audience, is absent or, at best incidental. Rhetoric, now a neglected art, falls somewhere between this and the drama, and can create a communal response. Some kinds of sculpture and painting on a monumental scale also come close to this kind of dramatic power over groups.

The borderlines are not as sharp as might at first be supposed, and this is demonstrated vividly by the baroque style which, in its most inspired moments, blurs the lines to such an extent that we can move from painting to sculpture to architecture to the music that fills those exotic spaces, and find it literally impossible to state exactly where one art ends and another begins. Nor is there any sharp distinction in style between a church, a palace, a theater, or a temporary masque setting, or whether the billowing draperies be of velvet or silk instead of marble. Equally unimportant, it seems, to the character of a style essentially dramatic, is whether the "happening" is a mythological scene or a Solemn High Mass, and whether it is presented on a ceiling, in a sanctuary, or on a lawn. The baroque is the supreme example of the *Gesamtkunstwerk* that Wagner wanted, a sophisticated happening so complete in its fusion of the arts as almost to bemuse the senses.

This kind of impact has been the aim of many modern artists as they deliberately break down the sense-categories into which we normally organize our impressions so that the spiritual energy has a greater chance to get through the defenses of reason and prejudice. "Soft sculpture" creates in useless, half-inflated plastic balloons the forms of such hard and utilitarian objects as typewriters and lavatory seats. Pictures are made up of photographs, newspaper cuttings, bits of stuff, and solid things like buttons. Musicians wear odd wigs or appear half-naked. "Op" art dazzles and confuses the eye, and actors sit on audiences' laps. The shock occasioned by this shows how set our ideas have become. Yet the old-fashioned pantomime took audience participation for granted, drew the audience into its bawdy confidence, exchanged crude jokes with individuals and invited them onto the stage. Shakespeare's audiences were quite accustomed to participating as a Roman crowd or an English army, and being ranted at by the despairing hero or cajoled by the apologetic fool (apologetic with reason, since the audiences were near enough to throw eggs or worse if they were not pleased).

There is one other borderline case which will be important to the theme of this book, and that is the "gospel"—a literary form that is explicitly an announcement, a dramatic and moving message. It is not intended primarily for private reading but for public presentation, and indeed private Scripture reading was not customary in the early Church. It was drama, involving an audience.

So we come back to the drama in its most introspective and yet embracing sense, and find here the means to discover more clearly the moving spirit of man in the event of salvation.

CHAPTER 1

The Raw Material

HERE is an account at first hand of the release of a powerful energy which, from all the evidence, is not an occasional freak but a constant element in human nature, though not often experienced so violently and explicitly. It is the terrifying frenzy of the Bacchae possessed by their god; the mysterious inflowing power of the Voodoo initiation; the weeping, laughing, ecstatic climax of conversion in a meeting of "Jesus people." Interpretations given to it by those who feel it may differ, and the results may be sometimes diametrically opposed to each other, but the type of energy released is the same. This is the raw material of man's transformation, the stuff that can change him.

It was the actor who played Puck in Peter Brook's now

famous 1970 production of *A Midsummer Night's Dream* who told John Kane, a reporter of the London *Sunday Times*, what some of the early rehearsals were like. The actors playing the Spirits were to be omnipresent in the play, to pervade it, and stamp it with their special character:

They were free to wander where they pleased and assist or screw up whatever they liked. It soon became obvious that the Spirits that morning were certainly mischievous, if not downright malevolent. The forest and its inhabitants exuded a primitive savagery that infected everyone who came into contact with them. As the group feeling grew, a wild gaiety seized the company. With books in one hand and a hoop or a cushion in the other, we whipped the play along like some frantic bobbing top until it eventually exploded during the Titania/Bottom confrontation in a welter of torn newspaper, cardboard phalluses and Felix Mendelssohn. As the noise and laughter died away, we looked around the room and, as though awakening from a dream ourselves, we realised that we had been possessed by some wild anarchic force, that we had been in contact with elements of the play that no amount of discussion or carefully plotted production could have revealed.

It is no accident that this particular play was the *Dream*, which is about sprites, fairies, spirits—the psychological underworld of earth's inhabitants who represent that side of human nature which it is, on the whole, necessary and convenient to disbelieve in. They are one aspect of the transforming power, and in this form it is anarchic, amoral, and unpredictable, though wildly exciting. It is tempting for the Christian to distinguish different manifestations of this force, and to say that the energy of the Bacchic revel must be of a totally different kind from the power that swept into the apostles in the upper room, or that suddenly illumines the minds and hearts of the quiet seekers after truth. It seems more likely that it is only the channels through which it works that are different, for these are constituted by the particular human environment, by individual character, by religious and cultural backgrounds; or by relationships, conscious choices, and particular (even ephemeral) feelings and opportunities. The setting, the results, the language, and the kind of behavior that express and define these for most people provide ways of deciding whether the experience of the release of elemental power is good or bad, creative or destructive.

But the force itself is indefinable, basic, the raw stuff of human *being*. Such a "happening" as described above releases it for a while. But what then? It has as an experience no *meaning*, nor can it last. People "wake up," as these actors did. Brook's own comment confirms this: "It had an extraordinary force and interest," he said, "but like all happenings it can never be repeated—it was there once and gone." What use is it, then? Its use is as precisely what it is —raw material. Once people have felt it, become aware of it as part of themselves, they can use it, not with complete control at first, but it is available. In this case, Brook's interpretation of the play required that his actors must never be allowed to forget that they were playing in the context of continual stage "happenings," a world "swift as a shadow, short as any dream." He was using the spontaneous experience, though triggered off semi-deliberately, to provide the type of awareness that could then be carefully and consciously exploited within the highly disciplined structure of the play. So we get the most extreme form of group and individual control and planned coordination combined with the power of personally and communally experienced anarchic force. By this combination it becomes no longer anarchic but purposeful and organized, yet *without loss of real power.* No wonder this production caused such a stir, both of enthusiasm and of anger, and both for the same reason.

Here, in a theatrical production, people were brought into violent and intimate contact with the phenomenon that concerns us here—the raw stuff that can finally be, equally, salvation or damnation, total life and fire and glory or total self-consuming destruction and hate. And we can see that the stuff itself is violent, powerful, and strange. This is, after all, what one should expect, but we have learned to think of the human soul as almost a blank, to be filled by good or evil. Yet, as the parable of the seven devils shows, it is unnatural and dangerous for the human "home" to be emptied. The not-at-all neutral character of the human raw stuff is indicated by the very word "salvation." We need to be saved or rescued—the human stuff is in danger—and that rescue is what the "play" is about.

The play is about salvation, and for centuries there have been two quite different ways of thinking about it. One is most familiar to traditional "church" Christians and is expressed in the notion that the Christian's duty on earth is to save his soul. This means, in simple terms, that he must live in such a way as to avoid the danger of damnation. It is, at least in its psychological emphasis, something that a man or woman must personally do, work at, achieve. Even though the theology behind it emphasizes that only God's free grace makes virtue possible, this is not really carried through in the application of the idea, for although the need to repent and the assurance of forgiveness is reiterated, this is seen mainly as admitting failure to achieve the requisite standard of conduct and getting divine help to try again. The emphasis is active and practical, and the important moment is the moment of death, when salvation is obtained—or not. To be saved means to die in a state of virtue (or at least of repentance for failure to be virtuous) and so receive the reward of virtue.

The other notion of salvation has been a theological undercurrent in Christianity from the time when the increasing institutionalization of the Church in Europe made the practical and active reward-of-virtue notion of salvation the simple and prevailing one. Many Christians reacted against it, feeling uneasy about it in some degree. This is not surprising, since it gave no scope for the use of that powerful "raw material" but rather tended to suppress it. The reaction sometimes took the form of the development of special forms of Christian life, more openly dependent on God and dedicated to seeking union with him. This could still be interpreted as "gaining heaven," and it was; but the *feel* of it, at its best, was quite different. The eremetical or monastic life, or the mystical life of any individual Christian, meant that salvation was experienced as something God did, even if the popular phrases and images kept the emphasis on human endeavor. Sometimes the desire to recapture the sense of salvation as God's work led to separation from the main body of the—by now politically-minded—Church. Most of the medieval sects were looking for experience of salvation in God, not dependent on human effort—and very weird some of them were, as we should expect, remembering that *Dream* rehearsal. But the best of them were striving to recover a theological reality that had never been denied but that was, in practice, without effect in the lives of most ordinary Christians.

They were trying to do what Peter Brook's rehearsal did for his actors, who were able to experience for themselves the thing they were about to try to present on the stage. This was something that the conventional stage had not directly attempted, though it assumed the existence of this power and saw evidence of it in great performances by actors whose training and approach was by the practice of physical and intellectual routines. In the same way, the official Church recognized evidence of the spirit at work in outstanding Christians, though their training was according to well-defined rules of conduct consciously pursued.

Eventually, therefore, the Reformation, politically motivated and mixed up though the issues were, saw opposing forces drawn up to fight over the nature of salvation. But the most familiar form of the second—experienced—notion of salvation only became a widespread and accepted Christian style with the rise of the evangelical movement in the late eighteenth and nineteenth centuries. The evangelicals demanded clear experience of conversion, and their question was: "Are you saved?" One knew when one was saved. It wasn't the end of the story; there was much struggle and ardor involved in maintaining the grace of conversion to the final deathbed scene beloved of evangelical biographers and storytellers—but it was crucial. But this sense that salvation comes at a certain definable moment during life and is wholly the work of God (though the person must pray ardently for it and strive to be worthy by purity of life) marks the recognizable division between the two main Christian notions of salvation. This, in its turn, reflects not just the conflict of opposed theological citadels but the basically different ways in which people think about the nonmaterial aspect of their lives. This difference can also be seen reflected in the development of dramatic experience—as has already been suggested.

These two notions of what salvation means are still associated with the two main Christian traditions, the Catholic and the Protestant. Historically, the difference is important and clear, but just because these have been historically— that is, in real political and social fact—associated with two streams of tradition, the two ideas have themselves been colored by historical events and needs. The very clarity of the Reformation conflict between faith and works was due as much to political as to theological factors. Luther was trying to recapture the Gospel sense of utter dependence on God's free grace. He saw this endangered by a Church too sure of its prerogatives and so anxious to control the means of grace as almost to see itself as a substitute for personal response to God. But we still suffer the consequences of the fact that Luther, and those who felt as he did, provided the German Princes with a remarkably convenient excuse for rejecting the political power of the papacy.

The pope, on his side, and those whose interest it was to support him, naturally found in themselves a strong need to uphold Catholic doctrine against the heretics, since their possessions and privileges were bound up with the papal power.

For in spite of their intransigence both traditions have always recognized both aspects of salvation. The Catholic tradition emphasized the Church as the *locus* of faith, the guide of the faithful in the understanding of what is required for salvation, and the provider of sacramental and corporate support on the long journey toward death—the moment of truth. But Catholic theology always emphasized also the nature of God's grace as a free and undeserved gift, bestowed in Baptism and fostered by Christian living. Catholic spirituality always recognized the existence of a conversion experience, though it regarded it as comparatively unusual and certainly not essential to salvation.

It is noticeable that when post-Reformation Catholic spirituality, frantically stressing whatever the reformers denied, emphasized obedience, good works, and the efficacy of the sacraments—even with only minimum good will on the part of the recipient—the Church's *culture* unconsciously tried to redress the balance. The more objective and legalistic the theory of Catholic spirituality became—expressed in endless examinations of conscience, set prayers, formal meditations, and a plethora of charitable organizations to channel the good works of Christians—the more the popular practice of it made use of every kind of psychological means to induce a subjective experience of religion. The extravagant emotionalism of baroque art; the richness of organ, polyphonic, and instrumental music; incense; rich colors and embroidery; and the almost mesmeric quality of high ritual helped to convey to the worshiper a sensible experience of the numinous by means essentially dramatic.

The spate of "devotions"—to the Sacred Heart, to the Mother of God under various titles, and to various saints—was directed entirely to stirring up feelings of repentance, of compassion for the suffering Christ, and of personal love for God. Although confessors warned their penitents against placing value on feelings of consolation, the response to such things as the apparitions at Lourdes in the middle of the nineteenth century, and to the cult of St. Therese of Lisieux at the end of it, showed the enormous need that ordinary Catholics had for an *experience* of salvation, for the sense that God was perceptibly present in human life in its everyday course and not just at the end of the journey. The hunger was very great. Vast crowds of peasants and small tradesmen gathered in the valley of the river Gave when the news spread that Bernadette's Lady was going to appear to her once more, and perhaps show herself to others as well.

This was only partly sensation-seeking. Much more, it was the unquenchable feeling of ordinary, not very good, Christians that God can transform lives, break through the shell of everyday-ness and bring to birth a new consciousness, an ecstasy of knowledge. They have been coming to Lourdes on the same quest, and in ever-increasing numbers, ever since, and for many the quest has not been fruitless.

At this point, the Catholic crowd is scarcely to be distinguished from the crowds that gathered round Wesley, and that now flock to listen to Billy Graham and, in a different vein, to crowd the enclosures of pop concerts or sit at the feet of the latest Eastern guru. All are seeking a direct experience of God's presence and grace, something that will change and transform, that will rescue them from doubt and dull hopelessness and the complex of negative attitudes and reactions. They want, in fact, salvation. And with the exception of a few extreme and evanescent sects, the Christian tradition, which sets crucial value on this once-for-all experience, also demands that it prove itself in daily conduct, in perseverance in right-doing and obedience to God until the moment of death brings final confirmation of the divine election.

Here we come to a theme which is crucial in every sense. The very self-controlled and rationalized stoic may persuade himself that the end of human life is a stopping and no more, but this is a highly artificial and precarious conviction. Whether it appears as the ultimate fear or the final triumph, or as an obscure and lurking ghost, the significance of the moment of death is overwhelming for everybody. The whole notion of salvation is bound up with it, and the two main concepts of salvation have death at their heart. So at this point, even so early in this study, we come up against the fact and experience of death, what people make of it, and how they think of salvation in relation to it. What we find, when we examine religious reactions to death and dying, is a *dramatic* structure. It is an event which, in the minds of religious people, gives scope for the release of that frightening and violent and unpredictable power we saw at work in the group of actors. But the important thing to notice is that at this moment in human life there is a tacit understanding among all concerned that this raw spiritual stuff must be subjected to proper control—and this control is that of drama.

As in a stage production, a "happening" will not do because it has no meaning by itself. It acquires a meaning when the energy is released within the bounds of an accepted and credible dramatic form. It is noticeable that people who deny that death has any particular meaning are at pains to suppress the dramatic aspects of it, because these give it meaning. The reluctance to warn the dying, the refusal to let children attend funerals or even know about death, the avoidance of the dying by relatives, and the propaganda for euthanasia—"dying with dignity" means, in this context, dying with a speed and reticence convenient to the survivors—all show that the recognizably dramatic forms of deathbed behavior are an assertion of death's meaning and importance.

To the evangelicals, as also to all groups whose way of life was consciously centered in God, the deathbed mattered because it was proof to all—especially to as many as could squeeze in to witness it—that salvation was real. It really had so taken hold of a person that he or she, cleansed of all lower affections, was entering into the final glory first glimpsed at the moment of being saved. The evangelical emphasis on death is paralleled in medieval and later Catholic accounts of martyrdom, or of the passing of holy people. In Catholic monasteries of men or women, the death of a member of the community is attended by all, and surrounded with prayer and a certain awed curiosity, as well as hope and joy. Perhaps there is sometimes an element of desire for morbid "kicks," as in people rushing to the scene of an accident, but this is not central any more than it was in the evangelical deathbed scenes that a later age, scared stiff of the whole subject, finds so repellent.

The Wesleyan gloating over dead bodies was partly didactic and sprang from a desire to impress the flighty or half-hearted with the fearful inevitability of dissolution. But even if we find the language exaggerated and the sentiments alien, it is impossible to read a genuine account of an evangelical deathbed, a Catholic account of martyrdom, or some other "edifying" death, without realizing that there is more here than a sadistic wallowing in the physical symptoms of a human being *in extremis*. There is a real sense of sharing in a hard but glorious process of final liberation. The dying person is about to discover what has always been, obscurely, present and active. These last moments can perhaps provide much needed encouragement and confirmation for those still on the way; and in their turn they feel they are helping, actively supporting the final struggle. Hence the close attention paid to every word and gesture of the dying person, the constant hope of some message of encouragement, some clear sign of the victorious conclusion.

We refer to these quite normally as "deathbed scenes." There is a certain mockery implied, a hint that a show is being put on to impress an audience, but it is the mockery not the scene that is misplaced. For, whether or not we accept the evangelical interpretation of human development, the evangelicals were right in supposing that attendance at such an event is a participation in what is happening. But this participation is of a special kind. The bystanders are not going to die, neither are most of them needed in a practical way. They are an "audience" and are important not only for what they themselves experience of emotional and spiritual cleansing or illumination, but also because they have a role to play. The chief actor, the dying person, *needs* the audience; he needs to feel them there. There is a communication going on between actor and audience that is important to both. Those who are more intimately concerned with helping the dying person in some capacity— doctor, minister, nurse, wife, husband, and so on—are, in some degree, also actors. They have a direct role in relation to the dying person, who, in many cases, cannot manage without them. It can happen, in fact, that one of them will prove to have the leading role if the dying person is, for instance, too ill to speak or very much in need of moral support. And this group is definitely separated from the audience, because each one has something definite to do other than just being there. There is, of course, an ambiguity here which does not normally occur in the theater (though some theaters try to introduce just this ambiguity) because some of the audience may be called upon to play an active role, or one of the actors may have nothing left to do and become audience. The distinction is clear, however, and so is the essentially dramatic character of the whole event.

It is not only dramatic in the loose sense, that it is moving and out of the ordinary; it is dramatic in the strict sense, that a conscious drama is being enacted. It is deliberate, not accidental. The "cast" know what they are about and even have a "text," in the sense that their religious tradition supplies them with particular words to describe and comment on what is happening. The role of each is laid down by custom, the unfolding of the drama toward its climax is understood and expected. We can realize how true this is if we imagine one of the "cast" failing to follow the "script." For instance, if the sorrowing wife suddenly announced that she couldn't sit there all day, there was washing to be done; or if the dying person sat up and demanded a boiled egg. Neither of these is altogether unlikely or very reprehensible, but the sense of shock is considerable. The play has been changed; it is comedy, not tragedy. More precisely, it is no longer about salvation but about getting on with everyday life.

We may approve of this shift; indeed many modern playwrights have used just this kind of shift to explode what they feel is a false drama, a scene carried through according to custom but without the vital participation that makes it an experience of genuine spiritual worth. Shaw, in *Major Barbara* and in *The Devil's Disciple*, exposed the explicit salvation-drama cliché, but the device is not confined to exposing the unreality of overtly religious situations. It is a traditional means of unmasking hypocrisy. And we know at once whether the shift in mood is really the pricking of a pretentious bubble, or merely evidence of boorish insensitivity to the real nature of what is happening. Both these reactions, however, show that we are aware of the inherently dramatic nature of a deathbed scene.

It is clear that death is not necessarily dramatic in this sense; it becomes so when those involved are consciously aware of a significance beyond the obvious physical facts and respond and react to each other accordingly.

After this, it may seem less strange to use a dramatic performance as a means to understanding so great a thing as man's achievement of an eternal destiny. It would seem altogether normal to cultures accustomed, as ours no longer is, to drama as an essential part of worship and of religious initiation and progress. Ritual is a form of dramatic presentation, and some kinds of ritual actually include the kind of story-enactment which we most easily think of as happening on a stage. It is a long way from the three vested clergy who represented for medieval congregations the three Marys at the tomb on Easter Sunday to the naturalistic stage presentations of this century. But there is a continuity, and the last thirty or forty years have shown (only among a few, at first) a more conscious rediscovery of the role of drama as a quasi-religious act having a power and a significance extending beyond the immediately beautiful and entertaining.

The drama, therefore, provides not only an apt image of the events of salvation as we experience them, it also provides an actual example of those happenings at a certain level. The purpose of this book is to see how that works.

I said earlier that the "play" is about salvation, and that the production of this play involves, as any play does, the stimulation of the essential raw material and its harnessing in dramatic structure. We saw at once how the deathbed scene shows this in action. But we also saw that there have been two schools of thought about how this raw material is best handled; which both fail significantly to be totally consistent—fortunately, since experience shows that neither emphasis is wholly true to the facts. So, before going further, I am going to bring on one of Christianity's great "dramatists," perhaps the very greatest, to take a bow. St. Paul is the one who really did manage to express the essential dramatic paradox with which this book is concerned. This paradox is that the "stuff" of salvation is anarchic, violent, formless, and amoral. Its potentiality is beyond description or grasp, yet it can only achieve that potential by means that are conscious, limited, formal, articulate, and highly disciplined. Yet all this discipline and form is irrelevant to the final achievement. Paul provided a language—rich, precise, flexible, and full of echoes—which has ever since been used to express the nature of this essential drama. In order to define the theme, then, and discover a little of the action it commands, we need to consider his vision of salvation and the words and images he used to express it.

The apparently accidental cultural combination which was Paul's milieu, plus his peculiar personal history, was exactly right for the man who was to shape Christian ideas about salvation. He had a strict Jewish background, a cosmopolitan experience in his Roman-ruled hometown, and an overwhelming nonritual conversion experience. In his own person, therefore, he combined the Jewish notion of salvation, as the result of long-term faithfulness and obedience to the Covenant, and the new Christian experience of total rebirth—the two main emphases ever since, as we have seen. Paul's brilliant mind, and his later very wide experience of coping with the new churches, combined to force him into finding words for the synthesis of these contradictory notions. He is often obscure, at first sight, because he was struggling to express *what had never been expressed before.* It is important to bear this in mind, for familiarity with his teaching easily makes it seem routine. It was, in fact, revolutionary.

His great theological breakthrough was his conception of the relation between the life of sin and the life that Christ won. To use such phrases, in one sense, immediately falsifies what Paul did, because the sad thing is that in spite of all he could do our notions of sin and grace are mostly very unPauline. We tend to think of sin as bad action, a failure to follow God's law and guidance, a turning away from truth. We think of grace and eternal life in confused images, sometimes as a sort of injection of holiness, sometimes as a reward to be won by obedience, sometimes as a kind of spiritual blood-transfusion—like the change of blood given at birth to a jaundiced Rhesus-factor baby, who is unable to survive with the blood with which he was born. This is an oversimplification, of course, but there is no doubt that few Christians habitually make use of the broad and yet sophisticated concepts that Paul developed in trying to educate his (on the whole) not very subtle converts.

Paul conceived of salvation as the coming into being of what God intended man to be, the glorious completeness of creation. It was not an added-on extra, or a present for the well-behaved, or something alien that changed the natural man into the supernatural. For him, there was always the double vision of the intended glory demonstrated by the triumph of the man Jesus, "the first born among many brethren," and the misery and shame of man as he had made himself through disobedience, enclosed in fear and loneliness, vitiated in body and mind, fettered, and blind.

For Paul, both sin and salvation are complete states of human life. Sin entered into the world when man began to think he could manage quite nicely without God's guidance, his very godlikeness making him believe in his power to order all things according to his own innate wisdom. The Greek word *sarx,* that Paul uses to refer to the resulting condition, has been translated "flesh," which would be perfectly satisfactory if we hadn't come to associate the word almost exclusively with sexual sin. When Paul talks about being "in the flesh" or about "works of the flesh," he is not talking about sex or even, by association, about the body as a sinful thing because it has sexual appetites. He means, rather, the human condition of limitation by a fleshly existence, with all the weaknesses and inadequacies that we know as part of bodily life. It is an odd and personal usage, and it is important to understand it because it expresses the subtle and realistic grasp that Paul had of man's condition. He did not consider the body to be evil (he used a different word to talk about the body as such), but rather as *subject* to evil in its present condition. This condition of being "in the flesh" means that man, turned away from God, has only his own resources to rely on, so that he is, in practice, *incomplete.* Not because he hasn't "got what it takes" but because the essential raw material is in an unavailable or wasteful form —rather like proteins in food that haven't the right balance of enzymes for the body to make use of them.

Yet man, in his proper being, is at one with God and his fellow men, so much so that to isolate the individual is to re-duce his humanity to an extent comparable with the dif-ference between an intelligent person and a congenital idiot. Both are human, but one is so incomplete that some hesitate to admit his humanity. Just as the idiot is a pathetic and usually repulsive object, so is man "in the flesh" in comparison with his proper state. He is isolated, not only from God but, because of that, from other human beings, and also from real self-understanding.

To put it differently, man is made to be essentially one with God, and this oneness is what develops his own human spirit. The unusableness of this oneness at the heart of him-self leaves him virtually dead—"dead in sin" is what Paul calls it. He lives on, because, in fact, God does not desert him; but it is a darkened, fearful, puzzled half-life. Given this Pauline insight, it is not so hard to see the structure of what we experience. People have a craving, as deep and genuine as the physical craving for food, for the realization of that essential oneness in some way that can be identified. It is no use having vague, violent feelings—a nostalgia for nothing in particular, a jealousy of nobody special. One wants to pin down the desire, the craving, and satisfy it; yet the very violence of the craving makes people afraid to discover its roots. We try to satisfy it with anything that can stop the ache for a bit. When it doesn't stop, we look around for someone to blame. Suspicious because ignorant, angry because helpless, reckless because without hope, servile through fear—this is man "in the flesh" as Paul sees him. And he lists the resultant "works of the flesh"—as we know them from experience—"fornication, gross indecency and sexual irresponsibility, idolatry and sorcery, feuds and wrangling, jealousy, bad temper and quarrels, disagreements, factions, envy, drunkenness, orgies, and similar things."

If we are tempted to feel that this is a rather puritanical list of what is evil in human behavior, we can ask ourselves whether this is how people behave when they have really found happiness. The answer is obvious. We condone or even encourage such things because we see them as ways to escape unhappiness, and therefore as often very understandable. But that is precisely Paul's point. This is that violent "stuff" of the human spirit driven in the wrong way. The body itself is affected and suffers sickness and death because it is not under the control of the divinely instilled wisdom. Man doesn't understand himself, not even his physical self, and both body and mind are distorted and morbid.

It is a depressing picture, and because of it Paul has been accused of being an antilife puritan, seeing man as essentially vile. But he has constantly emphasized the terrible damage that man's self-inflicted punishment has done, because he wanted to show up, by contrast, the extraordinary transformation that Christ makes possible. The Saviour does not merely forgive sin, he makes man realize what that violent raw material is able to be if only he will open himself to the power of the spirit. For this spirit of Christ is man's own human spirit, as well as God's spirit. It is as if human beings were "plugged in" to God, and through the inflowing of power and light can be set free from the life of the flesh and develop in themselves the life of the spirit.

Christ the Saviour is there as proof that the final liberation involves the total transformation of body and soul "in the spirit," as God intended man to be. The risen Christ is the proof that this is possible, the pledge of the reality of what is already happening when men turn to him in faith as Saviour. This idea will provide us with a key to the dramatic form of salvation in which Christ is both subject and player.

At this point we have to understand clearly that Paul recognized two ways of trying to repair the damage done by man's self-isolation. For there is another, also much misunderstood, Pauline concept—that of the Law, which came in to try to cope with life "in the flesh." It fades into insignificance before the power of Christ, the fully realized human spirit which inspires right conduct, not out of fear or a sense of duty but out of a fiery love that leaves no trace of other considerations, however worthy. Yet it is only the stringent discipline of the stage that makes a play possible at all.

"Law" is a universally encountered development. It has not only Paul's strict sense of the Jewish code promulgated in the heroic days of the people's history, but it also has the wider sense (which he recognized explicitly) of any culture's attempt to understand and regulate its behavior, and we see it in the essential disciplines of dramatic work. This is not just a matter of making conscious legal or other rules, it is the whole complex of custom, taboo traditions, and what might be called etiquette—the minor, commonly accepted regulations of any particular way of life. Much of all this arises gradually, without conscious intention, to meet particular needs. The conventions of some theatrical traditions, such as the Japanese "No" theater, are easily recognized examples of something that is less recognizable in wider and vaguer contexts.

The relationship between law and salvation is a subtle one, as we shall see. Paul may sometimes seem to make the contrast too glaring, but he had his reasons. The totally "other" nature of the event of salvation is hard to grasp, and there has been a disastrous tendency throughout Christian history to try to reduce salvation to the observance of law. (We can see the same tendency in the theater.) Paul had to battle with this when the Judaizers among the first Christians tried to make salvation depend on the keeping of the old Jewish law in detail. This battle has been necessary ever since, for it is usually only a matter of a few years before some attempt to rediscover the "liberty of the children of God" becomes in its turn merely a newly conceived compulsion to adhere to a particular life-style. (Would a troupe of dedicated experimental actors welcome a recruit from traditional repertory or make any attempt to consider his ideas seriously?)

Thus the vivid experience of actors in rehearsal brings the Pauline paradox before us in a perfectly recognizable form. It is not a religious experience, but it is the stuff that can become a religious experience if the context gives it religious description and channels the results into religious types of behavior. The combination of spontaneous "happening" and carefully planned context for its exploitation is not at

all new in man's religious history. It is almost routine in certain kinds of religion, in fact, and these are chiefly unofficial
ones. Religions that make use of such expected outbreaks of
energy are not necessarily underground or subversive sects.
However, the Adamites, the Brethren of the Free Spirit, and
other medieval secret sects in their various forms, are examples of cases where the need for secrecy and the sense of
being among the few enlightened ones created an atmosphere favorable to the unleashing of demonic power. Such
outbreaks occur also in sects that are quite "respectable"
but that are still minority cults, not having the character of
an established religion but helping to satisfy needs unhelped
by official cult forms.

Mithraism in the later Roman Empire, and around the
same time the cult of Isis as a Roman revival, are examples
of this, and the early evangelical movement among the new
industrial poor in England and America fulfilled the same
need. In some African tribal religions, the official form of
religion may have the same character, inducing outbreaks
of trance, illumination, or ecstasy in initiates, and this may
be because the precariousness of normal life has the same
isolating effect as that of being a minority. In some situations, just to be human feels like being a threatened elite,
because nature itself, and the world of untameable spirits
that possesses and moves it, seems the ruling power against
which man has to struggle. The Eskimos, always at the
mercy of a relentless and violent climate, and the West Indian slaves and their descendants whose threatened situation was created by political and economic forces, are in the
same situation psychologically. In these and similar cases
the basis of religion is the power of individuals and groups

to experience the outbreak of the elemental power in themselves, whatever its origin or nature is supposed to be.

The link between this type of situation and the group of actors discovering together a kind of Dionysiac ecstasy is not that the actors were oppressed but that they, too, were removed from normal life and its moral and social motivations. Ordinarily, in the interests of practical needs, such feelings have to be kept out of the way in the subconscious.

In the case quoted, there was a predisposing mood of adventure and enquiry, an isolating effect of being in rehearsal and removed from all other concerns. There was also the more immediate disruptive influence of the deliberately licensed spirits whose job was precisely to remove the usual props to conscious behavior by their use of practical joke techniques and disconcerting and upsetting tricks of many kinds. Their function was that of the "Lords of Misrule," whose job at the medieval Christmas festivities was to goad and provoke people out of everyday decorum and into an anarchic wildness and joy. At the rehearsal, the "Lord of Misrule"—in fact if not in action—was the director himself; a sort of high priest controlling but not joining in the release of the forces he needed for his purposes. His equivalent of a temple, a cave of mysteries, or a remote forest clearing is a stage. In that particular case it was a stage designed like a white and inescapable prison cell, remote from any associations with everyday life. And in this strange setting the released power was marshaled and exploited and had its effect—a *dramatic* effect, since that is the nature of such an experience.

The same thing happens when a powerful preacher works on the minds of groping and spiritually hungry people and releases an ecstasy of joy and a sense of boundless freedom. Having helped to release it, the evangelist's job is then to direct it, calling on the conscious mind of the convert to use his new power in the service of God and man, according to his "script"—certain well-established patterns and examples, defined in particular forms of words, both in description and in the language of worship. Then the answer to the old question: "Are you saved?" will be "yes"—meaning that this experience has been undergone and understood and acted upon.

Yet, as we have seen, the power thus experienced is not necessarily beneficial in its effects. It can be ephemeral, destructive (unleashing violence), or defiant (bent on demonstrating freedom from moral and social restraint)—a sort of children's revolution. Is this really the stuff of man's transformation, the power of the spirit to create a new heaven and a new earth?

If I am right, and it is the context that determines the nature of the outbreak of the one and constant power, then we need not be surprised at the almost shocking varieties of result. Again, the drama can throw a disconcertingly clear light on this kind of experience of spiritual power. Another comment on the same production of the *Dream*, this time from the veteran critic of the *Sunday Times* Harold Hobson, shows very clearly the ambiguous nature of the forces at work. Here, once more, we can see the thing working at several levels: the level of a particular interpretation of Shakespeare's play; the level of a theological exposition of the nature of the human predicament; the level of the actors' complicity with and service of the forces they are portray-

ing; and the level of the audience's involvement by sympa-
thy in what is, for them, a preaching or "happening," since
they are experiencing a new thing and it is telling them
things about their own inner selves.

Throughout the performance one feels that there is a Power,
prone to blundering and often malicious, but which on the whole
and finally leads to righteousness. . . . The Power which Mr.
Brook suggestively, and without direct statement, creates . . . is
not, like the Christian God, omnipotent and infallible. It is rich in
errors, it frequently bungles the task it sets itself, and it is essentially a divided kingdom. On it, however, depends the welfare of
humanity. So long as Oberon and Titania remain estranged, their
inharmony will be reflected in the ordinary world of men and
women, in which their attendants constantly interfere. This inter-
ference can be very frightening. The woods are coils of wire, and
when the fairies swing these wildly through the air like venomous
serpents to encircle Hermia, the sense of evil and of danger in the
theatre is very strong.

But there is never any doubt that eventually the evil will be
overcome. It is at the points at which it assures us of this that Mr.
Kane's playful and mocking Puck is at its best. At the worst of his
jealousy Mr. Howard's Oberon is never deserted by a high seri-
ousness that clearly sees the limits beyond which a humiliating
and painful joke must not be pushed, either upon earth or in a
world elsewhere. It is this that gives its great authority to his final
speech, in which, when all the tumult and the shouting and the
desperate distresses are over, Oberon lays on the house of Theseus
and Hypolita a solemn blessing. Mr. Howard is right to take the
speech slowly, as if every word had behind it the power of a god.
It is the climax towards which the whole play has been moving.
In it a god speaks, and a god should not be rushed.

Here we can see a baffling interlocking of meanings. The critic interprets the director who interprets the text which interprets the human predicament, using ancient symbols organized by a curious kind of partly Christian consciousness. But what Shakespeare was writing about was the human entanglement in sin which, as we saw earlier, is not just guilty actions but the whole web of fear and ignorance —fear and ignorance of each other, of the inner self, of the power to order and control it. Yet this power is within us; it pursues us, teases us, and guides us. Finally, if we let it, it blesses us.

Now this might be just Shakespeare's opinion, with no greater or lesser authority than, say, Shaw's notions about the morality of pacifism. But the fascinating thing is that the means of presenting this theological comment on the nature of human life is the same as the theme itself—that is, it rouses up the latent and transforming power in the actors, and it gives it "a local habitation and a name" in the sprites who run wild all one long night in that sacred and fearful point outside normality which is represented by midsummer's night. (Belonging neither to the first nor the second half of the year, it is a non-time, outside human reckoning, and therefore the arena for subversive power to seize its chance.) Yet, says Hobson, Brook, Shakespeare, and Christian theology, these elemental spirits—properly understood and used—are beneficent. It is good for us to be in this wood, made aware of the frightening powers within and about us, living dangerously on the fringes of knowledge, though not for too long. This way lies salvation.

But there is a long way yet to go. There is all of daily life to get through, a living to make, a mate to marry, children to rear, and a death to encounter at the end. No repetition of Bacchic liberation can transform this, and isolated experiences of this kind, even if repeated, still leave the rest of life untransformed. Does salvation mean waiting patiently for the final and lasting experience of what can only be glimpsed in single and separate moments? Must the lovers go back to the terrors of the forest to find again the bliss of reunion in the morning? Can the actors only make their full impact in moments of unpredictable "happening"?

We know this last is not so. We know that in dramatic work the released power can be translated and channeled without losing force—indeed with a great increase of power. And knowing this we can see immediately that when people reject anything unspontaneous or traditional in religion because it tends to dilute the primitive religious energy, they show a misunderstanding of the nature of spiritual power. It is also a frequent mistake to suppose that natural talent will be spoiled or made barren by the discipline of professional training. The opposite is the case, provided, of course, that it is the right kind of training.

This introduces consideration of the other notion of salvation: eternal life obtained by loving obedience in a way of life ordered to that end. The raw material of that final liberated life is considered to be present and active, its fruits are good and loving behavior, peace and unity in the common life, and patience to persevere. The sinful condition of human life is the obstacle to be overcome by deliberate discipline and training designed to free the channels of grace and subdue habits and ideas that interfere with its work. This means, in practice, that the Christian, or indeed any religious person, proposes to himself a role in keeping with the ultimate aim and tries to shape himself to fit it. He has, in fact, to study a role and work himself into it, and the role he is asked to play is that of Christ himself.

In the interview already quoted, Peter Brook also said something which is revealing in this connection: "It's from the inner life of the performer that the magic, the unfolding possibilities of the play, must emerge." This observation of an experienced and brilliant director, drawing on his knowledge of the dynamics of dramatic work, indicates the theological balance required. The "inner life of the performer" is his own, unique, personal raw material. In its raw state, as we saw, it has not necessarily a particular moral direction or spiritual significance. The role given to the performer provides this significance and direction. And the important thing to note here is that this happens not only when a director of unusual insight and courage dares to release the stuff in the raw and *then* discipline it; it also happens in the more traditional type of dramatic preparation, both remote and immediate, in which the actors begin by studying the techniques of their craft, and later the text of the play, and are expected to develop in rehearsal, by slow stages, a full intellectual and emotional understanding of the role they have to play.

Here we can already see how the necessary polarity of the dramatic event, requiring both the upsurge of the inner life and the painfully acquired techniques of the craft (the two are essentially incompatible yet both are absolutely required) reflects and, in fact, is part of the essential polarity of man's experience of the spirit.

In the following chapters I want to take different aspects

and relationships in the dramatic experience and, with their help, to illuminate some bits of theology which have become so familiar verbally that we often don't know what we are talking about.

CHAPTER 2

The Play

ONE of the traditions about salvation, as we have seen, concentrates greatly on the happening, the saving moment in the life of a human being. The experience of actors in the early stages of rehearsal, suddenly feeling the daemon of the play take hold of them, showed a significant resemblance to the conversion process. But the director of a play and the preacher of a mission cannot rely on such a moment of inner release; it requires two more things in order to be effective. One is some kind of preparation which makes the experience recognizable and therefore meaningful both to the person who experiences it and to those who form the group or community (of whatever nature) among whom it happens. The other is a follow-up in which the experience is made to power all future acts with a new and explicit purpose, and to guide and support them with a framework of discipline laid down by some kind of tradition or corpus of rules and practice, made appropriate to the purpose.

That sounds very general, and it has to be so, because conversions or illuminating experiences take place in so many different contexts. The group that preaches may be old and big and confident, with well-established yardsticks for measuring spiritual experience and time-tried recipes for developing it. Or it may be a new sect in revolt against all doctrine but inevitably making up new doctrines of its own as it goes along, and measuring its—and its converts'—experience more by their immediate intensity and emotional force than by their effects on normal behavior thereafter.

In the case of those newly converted from outside the group, the preparation leading up to the crucial experience may well be inexplicit, and consist mostly of that displacement and upsetting of normal securities described earlier, plus a real, if nebulous, desire for and openness to the experience. Thus, if we can imagine that group of actors joined by an outside person who had come in out of curiosity, or out of friendship for one of the actors, we could suppose that the common experience of possession by the elemental spirits might be shared by him, but not as transforming, only as interesting and enjoyable, or maybe disturbing. Unless he had already undergone some kind of interior preparation that made him sensitive to what was going on, he would remain a spectator, though he might be sufficiently moved for this to constitute a preparation for some kind of future experience of his own. The desire for transformation has to be present, even if scarcely recognized; without it the person is not eligible for a proper role in the play. We may think of God as the director of the drama of salvation, but also as the author of the play. We realize, then, that it is not enough for him to offer mankind the possibility of transformation out of the state of sin into that of glory. He has to provoke a desire for it, and that at a deeper level than a mere wish that things were better. Then he has to create a situation in which people will be prepared to follow out the directions of the spirit within them, and also to understand what is happening.

This is what has come to be known as "salvation history." Salvation history is history presenting itself to a group of people not as the record of dynastic achievement or victories in war, of progress in the arts of civilization or in technological expertise, but as the visible action of God demonstrating dramatically his care of mankind and his desire for its love and devotion solely in order to bring it to the fullness of perfection and joy. It is, in fact, history experienced as a drama, a deliberately organized and presented selection of actual past experience which therefore communicates a coherent and inherent message, and that message is of God's will to save and of the way this can happen.

All religious cultures have had some way of presenting the drama of salvation. Sometimes it has been mythical, and ritually presented, demonstrating that man's happiness lies in identifying with the internal drama of the community of the gods. Their loves and feuds, dangers and achievements have created the world, account for its history, and continue to have their effect on mankind. The worshiper can gain prosperity or virtue by understanding this, and by knowing how to move with the power of the divine actions. At a certain level this "moving with" can become the transforming experience in which the worshiper is no longer simply understanding and obeying but actually taking part in the divine drama. The shift is, in fact, from audience to actor, and we shall examine this shift later. At the moment I am mainly concerned to show the notion of salvation history as a drama enacted before the eyes of the human racc, presented in such a way as to teach men and women to understand truths about the nature of the relationship between God and man.

A good play has a shape. It must display the characters and their natures and tendencies, show the necessary development of their several natures in relation to each other, moving toward an expected but previously unguessed climax, whose consequences must then be shown, at least implicitly. A play in which the events are shown developing under their own steam, so that the characters are merely their necessary agents, is an unconvincing and dull play. Salvation history in the Jewish and Christian tradition is not a detective play whose sole value is in the solving of an intellectual puzzle. It is a play in which the course of events does visibly depend on the responses of the characters to each other and to the exterior events that overtake them. They have real choices, and their decisions shape the outcome, so that for the audience a large part of the tension of involvement arises from the knowledge that the choices could have been otherwise.

How nearly, after all, the fleeing Hebrews abandoned their enterprise and turned back from the terrors of the desert to the known, if harsh, life of captivity! The tussle of wills between Moses as God's spokesman and the sulky and reluctant ex-slaves forms an essential part of the development of the drama, and the same kind of conflict is a recurring feature of the whole history of the Chosen People. There was, in real life, much else—settlement of the land, development of a culture greatly influenced by its neighbors, learning of agricultural methods by a nomad people, diplomacy with other nations. These things appear incidentally; they are, or were, the scenery and props, but they are not part of the movement of the drama. The play is a play about love, about the wooing and winning of the stubborn human race in preparation for the coming of its Bridegroom, the Anointed, the Prince.

This is why the earlier story of the Hebrew people is an essential part of the Christian play. Without it, the nature of the salvation offered by Jesus would be impossible to understand fully. Indeed those Christian groups that have lost touch with the Old Testament as salvation history, and regard it simply as history and a source of moral instruction, tend to have a narrow understanding of the mission of Jesus himself. It is like coming to a performance of Shaw's *Pygmalion* at the point where Eliza has been presented to society. Her cockney origins being unknown to the late arrival, her subsequent behavior would make no sense and the resulting conflicts would seem inexplicable outbreaks of crazy, childish temper.

It is not enough to have a record of man's religious development, it has to be understood in a particular way, as drama with an inner dynamism in which the spectator is caught up as he follows its development. In the case of some Christian forms of heightened ritual, especially in the sects,

it is the sort of play in which the audience becomes so identified with the action that at the end they rise and pour onto
the stage, becoming part of the action of the drama itself;
and this not by accident but as a part of the play, a part
striven for by the director and actors in preparing the production. In other cases, such as Hindu temple dances, the
aim is less to produce a transforming or converting effect
than to share in a performance which is in some sense sacramental; that is, the act itself is effective as a prayer of adoration, propitiation, and so on. But there is often an element
of both characters, and this is so in the case of Judaism and
of the older Christian traditions.

There are innumerable examples in the history of religion of this kind of dramatic presentation, however conceived. According to their main aim, they vary from the
elaborate and detailed ritual dance-dramas of Bali, with
their subtly stylized movements and their rich and stun-
ningly beautiful costumes, to the vast revival meetings of
Billy Graham or the less respectable and much smaller versions staged by Jesus groups with deafening rock music,
chants, claps, and swaying of tranced bodies. These latter
two are not "scripted" beforehand and, therefore, the version of salvation presented is less explicit. This lack may
lead to peculiar results later when gaps in understanding
become apparent and are filled with such oddities as the
erotic religious poetry sent out from a secret hideaway by
David Moses, the leader of the group called the "Children
of God." But there is, in even such disparate examples, the
evidence of a common religious need to bring out the inner
impulses of the spirit and make them accessible as an exterior, sensible experience of a kind that the whole person can

respond to intellectually, emotionally, and spiritually—
though the balance of these vary.

The most illuminating, from the Christian point of view,
is the historical drama of the Passover ritual of Judaism. It
is, of course, not by any means the only important Jewish
feast. There are others, such as the feast of Tabernacles,
which vividly re-present an historical experience not only as
a memorial to past heroes but as the re-statement of national and spiritual character and identity resulting from
that event. When the people built huts of branches and
lived in them for a week, celebrating with many songs and
rituals and dances, they were not merely remembering the
desert wanderings of their fathers before they reached the
Promised Land, but were reaffirming in their common life
their continued dependence on the Lord who gave them
their homeland and who might take it away from a people
grown too self-confident and proud to acknowledge the contingency of human affairs. Judaism, unlike such other great
religions as Hinduism or the ancient cults of Greece and
Latin America, is essentially an historical faith whose whole
character depends on actual past events that gave the people their religious identity. The feasts of the year may have
originated in agricultural festivals of the same kind as those
of their neighbors, but they became linked to national history in a way that made them quite distinct in character
and purpose from those celebrated at Hazor or Ugarit.
Much of the ritual, religious style, and sanctuary design
were borrowed from such neighboring examples, however.

The Passover feast is not only the festival most obviously
relevant to Christians, but is also the crucial Jewish feast because it celebrates the event, or rather the whole dramatic

series of events, that created a Chosen People. The liberation from slavery was, in history and ritual, the starting point of a people with a salvation history and a salvation theology. But the commemoration of it is not the recital of an historical record but the presentation in symbolic form of the events and their saving significance, accompanied by dialogue, story, and song which explain and comment on the events.

What is the play about? It is about the struggle between Moses and Pharaoh for the liberty of a whole nation. It is about the passionate love of the people for their homeland. It is about God's miracles for his people in many periods, and it is about the nationhood of the people with all its traditions, its wise men, its sorrows and hopes.

It is about all these things, and that is why it is not an historical pageant but a real play, presented for a purpose and carrying meaning at several levels. The Jewish writer, Chaim Raphael, in his magnificent history of the Passover Haggadah, *A Feast of History,** puts it like this:

The Haggadah draws us into history in this way not only by the prayers and songs it contains, but through an evocation of the millions of Jews who have sat around the Seder table in countless generations, in infinitely varied circumstances, reciting these same words. But if the roll-call of our ancestors and contemporaries echoes, as it must, the story of man in all his manifold and colourful variety, the ceremony itself, geared to a "family" recital of our relationship with each other and with "the God of our Fathers," takes us finally back into our personal story. Prayers

---

* Chaim Raphael, *A Feast of History.* Weidenfeld and Nicolson/Arthur Barker Ltd/World University Library, London, England, copyright © by Simon & Schuster, Inc.

and memories flowing for thousands of years speak to us, at the Seder table, in terms of Jewish existence at this precise moment of history. We re-live the story of the Exodus as applying to ourselves: we have all come out of "Egypt"—out of Russia, out of Germany, out of the desperate crises that threatened the newly reborn Israel.

He reminds us of the way in which Jews celebrated the Seder through every kind of persecution, from the secret Passovers of Spain, when Jews risked the Inquisition to celebrate the Seder, to the last doomed Seder of the Warsaw Ghetto or those celebrated in Belsen and other concentration camps, and adds:

It must be that the strength of feeling in the Jewish experience has some objective staying power, justifying itself ultimately in positive, tangible form, where everything seems to be conspiring to smother it.

But the tangible form itself has a great deal to do with the staying power.

The yearly celebration of the way in which God saved the people and made them his own forever insures that these events do not remain a tradition only. The repeated drama re-creates the experience it recalls and tells and symbolizes. In this play, its meaning becomes clear, precise, and yet evokes a response at levels of both personal and communal life. Chaim Raphael says:

("Haggadah" means a "recital"—of the story of the Exodus; but it includes the whole mixture of folklore, prayer, ritual.) On the surface, the Passover Haggadah is merely the libretto for the

Seder, but is, in fact, a book of magic. *Why is this night different?* We know the answers in advance: we were slaves in Egypt, and God set us free; but we await the Seder each year, with mounting excitement as the night comes nearer, to hear history speak again. Ancient as the words of the Haggadah are, we know that we shall hear in them something which has been prepared for us alone. In one sense, time stands still: the ritual of the Seder is set out and followed as it has been, in essentials, for nearly two thousand years. But in another sense, the words have always been charged with fresh meaning for each generation by the situation and drama of the times.

"Time stands still." This phrase is used here to refer to the unchanging character of the Seder ritual through the centuries, but it has a larger meaning, for really effective drama, however topical, must stir depths in human nature which are eternal. The "moment in and out of time" is the point at which the human spirit, conditioned by time and the world, realizes that its essential being is not confined after all. The mystic's eternal now and the "sacred space" of ritual drama, are both realizations that historical sequence is a transient kind of reality, by definition—and not the only one. Paradoxically, it is the essentially historical drama of Exodus that creates the "moment in and out of time" of Passover. It can do this because it is a drama, a play with a specific subject and a prescribed text.

The Jewish people themselves wrote the text, under the prodding of judges and prophets and the stimulus of their own experiences. Although it was their own history they were remembering, it took many centuries and many conquests, apostasies, repentances and rescues before the meaning of it began to take shape in their minds in a way that could be set out as a permanent and traditional ritual, with the many levels of meaning to which Chaim Raphael refers. It was all this experience that finally made it clear that the play God wrote was not simply about the saving of a particular people and their formation as a people with an astonishing destiny, but also about the nature of the spiritual destiny of the human race.

It is at this point that the Christian contribution takes over and rewrites the play. The resonances of universal spiritual significance, present but not elaborated in the Seder ritual, are taken up by the New Testament writers and written into the text of the new play.

Over and over again the Exodus themes are taken up, quoted, and then transformed. They are not changed into something different; rather they are applied both more widely and more deeply. The Passover play, instead of being a yearly dramatic representation of the salvation of a nation from slavery, becomes a strange overlapping thing in which there are roles for all of mankind. Only a small number of people actually play the parts, yet their performance has a constant reference to those others who have not yet been, as it were, "auditioned."

In John's Gospel, the theology of the early Church is always conscious of this audience, which consists of potential actors. "The glory which thou has given me I have given to them," Jesus says, in what has been called the High Priestly prayer before his passion, "that they may be one even as we are one, I in them and thou in me, that they may become perfectly one, so that the world may know that thou has sent me and hast loved them even as thou hast loved me"

(John 17:23). The saved are made one as they have realized in themselves the nature of that raw material of the spirit, and have become more and more united as they learn to express in appropriate words and actions what they know and are discovering together of the drama of salvation. But this is not merely for their own benefit; it is explicitly done so that the world may know and be moved to recognize the reality of salvation.

The famous Good Shepherd passage makes it explicit that there are potential actors among those not of the fold of Israel: "And I have other sheep, that are not of this fold; I must bring them also, and they will heed my voice" (John 10:16). These others are to be invited to take part in the drama of salvation, and they are to be moved to do so by *seeing* it and *hearing* it acted out in and by those who have already known it. But how are men to call on him in whom they have not believed? And how are they to believe in him of whom they have never heard? And how are they to hear without a preacher? And how can men preach unless they are sent? This "sending" is part of the play of a salvation that discloses itself as essentially universal, which leads to a realization that the new play has several different scales in time and place. One scale is universal; the cast includes not only men and women but all creation, the very earth itself, in a cosmic salvation. First, "the creation waits with eager longing for the revealing of the sons of God," as if this time the nonhuman creation were the audience. But soon it is not audience but actor, joining in with the humans who have understood and taken their places in the drama: ". . . because the creation itself will be set free from bondage and obtain the glorious liberty of the children of God.

. . . We know that the whole creation has been groaning together until now, and not only the creation but we ourselves, who have the first fruits of the Spirit, groan inwardly as we wait for adoption as sons, the redemption of our bodies" (Romans 8:19–24).

Here, the whole earth is in the position of the enslaved Hebrews—"And the people of Israel groaned under their bondage and cried out for help, and their cry under bondage came to God" (Exodus 2:23).

But this cosmic scale is balanced by a realization that the drama is also on the scale of the inner spiritual experience of each one, without losing any of its universality. This is no longer a national salvation history but a drama of creation itself and also of each human soul. Paul's complex and subtle psychology is easy to misunderstand, because he elaborated a new terminology to explain the new revelation, and in doing so used words with changing associations. But one of his recurring preoccupations was what actually went on inside the person who heard the preaching and believed, and so was saved. And he knew (he could hardly help knowing) that this didn't mean a total transformation all at once. In a sense, the spiritual Exodus of each one is a continuing process: "But if Christ is in you, although your bodies are dead because of sin [this doesn't mean necessarily personal guilt but the general human condition of choosing the wrong things and hating and fearing, which affects human physical and psychological existence at every level], your spirits are alive because of righteousness. . . . For all who are led by the Spirit of God are sons of God. For you did not receive the spirit of slavery to fall back into fear, but you have received the spirit of sonship, . . . and if chil-

dren, then heirs. . . . heirs of God and fellow heirs with
Christ, provided we suffer with him in order that we may
also be glorified with him" (Romans 8:10; 14–17).

The slavery in Egypt is a continuing, personal, spiritual
experience, even though the new freedom is both promised
and actually experienced. This is hard to express but perfectly familiar in practice. The freedom is destined to be
completed in the Promised Land, the New Jerusalem. This
is drama on the scale of the single human soul, and it has its
cast of characters whom Paul names and moves around on
his human stage—Sin, Death, Law, Grace, Life. But these
characters also appear on the stage of man's history, and
here they are joined by Adam and Christ in a sort of symbolic ballet. And again, they appear on the smaller stage;
first Adam/Death and then Christ/Life ruling the action,
as we watch the results:

As one man's trespass led to condemnation for all men, so one
man's act of righteousness leads to acquittal and life for all men.

That is on the scale of man's whole spiritual history. Leaving aside here the involved question of the precise meaning
of Adam's sin and its "infectiousness," it is clear that the
drama worked out between these two characters has a universal significance. But the same passage later on shifts
without apology to the scale of the individual conscience:

Do you not know that all of us who have been baptized into
Christ Jesus were baptized into his death? We were buried with
him by baptism into death, so that as Christ was raised from the
dead by the glory of the Father, we too might walk in newness of

life. . . . We know that our old Self was crucified with him, so that the sinful body might be destroyed, and we might no longer be enslaved to sin . . . For we know that Christ being raised from the dead will never die again: . . . So you also must consider yourselves dead to sin and alive to God in Christ Jesus. . . . Do not yield your members to sin as instruments of wickedness but yield yourselves to God as men who have been brought from death to life; . . . for sin will have no dominion over you, since you are not under Law but under Grace (Romans 6: 8–14).

This is a long way from the many-leveled but essentially simple symbolism of the Passover salvation-history drama. Paul, Jewish through and through though he was, found himself unable to unfold the full implication of the new revelation of salvation purely in the words and symbols of the old. Indeed, he battered on the very limits of language in his attempts to express what he knew and saw in himself and others, and this is why he was driven to personify his concepts and to introduce them as new characters in the play.

Peter, with a less adventurous mind but a strong sense both of the stunning originality of the new play and of its essential roots in the old one, is much easier to understand. But he is also much less able to express the paradoxes and conflicts of salvation as it takes place in the human spirit. Because he is not trying to say so much, he makes the broad shape of the drama much clearer at first hearing.

(There has been a tendency among exegetes to regard with suspicion the strong evidence that it was Peter the Apostle who wrote the letters, because the Greek is accurate and idiomatic, and a fisherman from Galilee couldn't have done it. The middle-class arrogance of the assumption that a fisherman could not have a good mind or a gift for language is staggering. The letters, in fact, have a style in character with the Peter of the Gospels—simple but shrewd, straightforward, with a grasp of essentials and a lot of feeling but no taste for intellectual subtleties; a good teacher and organizer, not a poet or a theologian.)

Peter begins by bringing on the prophets of the Old Covenant, but he gives them lines very different from those they have in the Judaic version of the drama:

The prophets who prophesied of the grace that was to be yours searched and inquired about this salvation; they inquired what person or time was indicated by the Spirit of Christ within them when predicting the sufferings of Christ and the subsequent glory. It was revealed to them that they were serving not themselves but you, in the things which have now been announced to you . . . through the Holy Spirit sent from heaven, things into which angels long to look (I Peter 1:10–12).

Peter is presenting the salvation drama of the Old Testament in terms of the New, and he is here presenting it to the converts of the New Testament to encourage them in their own, still tentative, role-playing. But he places the action in the same position as that of the old version, only on a different plane—that is, the drama is the drama of a *people* (and this Paul makes much less clear) which has a continuity with the original People of God, not only because Jesus was of the Jews but because in character they are (Gentiles though they be), like the people of Israel, a "holy people" set aside to perform the drama of salvation:

As obedient children, do not be conformed to the passions of your former ignorance, but as he who called you is holy, be holy yourselves in all your conduct, since it is written, "You shall be holy, for I am holy" (I Peter 1:14–16).

The holiness does not consist in virtuous behavior (though virtue is required of the holy as fitting and proper), but in being set aside, "consecrated," to carry out a divine purpose of some kind. Peter then links this holiness of God's new people to the state of slavery from which they are saved, as the Israelites were, followed by a period of exile before the Promised Land is reached. The reference to the Passover lamb is explicit:

And if you invoke as Father him who judges each one impartially according to his deeds, conduct yourselves with fear throughout the time of your exile. You know that you were ransomed from the futile ways inherited from your fathers, not with perishable things such as silver or gold, but with the precious blood of Christ, like that of a lamb without blemish or spot (I Peter 1:17–19).

This Passover lamb suddenly provides the link to the wider scale of the drama which Peter has hitherto ignored, and having mentioned it, he drops the subject again:

He was destined before the foundation of the world but was made manifest at the end of the times for your sake. Through him you have confidence in God, who raised him from the dead and gave him glory . . . (I Peter 1:20, 21).

The real scene of Peter's version of the play is definitely not the cosmic one, nor yet the interior struggle, except in the sense of the straightforward moral effort to live up to the demands that holiness makes. His imagery all comes from

the Old Testament, and is interspersed with plain moral ex-
hortations—as if it were a director's instructions on how the
parts are to be played. The following passage includes direct quotations from Exodus and the prophet Hosea, and
ends with the only reference to the "audience" which appears, for Peter still *feels* the play as his ancestors did—one
that concerned primarily themselves. The Old Testament
does contain (especially the later books) the idea that Israel
has a world mission, but it was rather a speculation for theo-
logians and mystics, not an idea that took deep root in popular religion. Peter's religion was certainly popular, and his
recognition of the new people's responsibility to play for an
audience was real but not, evidently, a deep personal con-
cern:

But you are a chosen race, a royal priesthood, a holy nation,
God's own people, that you may declare the wonderful deeds of
him who called you out of darkness into his marvelous light. Once
you were no people but now you are God's people; once you had
not received mercy but now you have received mercy."
    Beloved, I beseech you as aliens and exiles to abstain from the
passions of the flesh that wage war against your soul. Maintain
good conduct among the Gentiles, so that in case they speak
against you as wrongdoers, they may see your good deeds and glo-
rify God on the day of visitation (I Peter 2:9–12).

    This shows how completely he identifies the old and new
People of God, for he was writing to Christians converted
from paganism; that is, Gentiles in the eyes of the Jews.
    These are a few passages out of the many which show
how the revelation in Christ was felt and expressed in essen-

tially dramatic ways, just as the revelation through Moses had been, on its narrower stage. This is not accidental, this is how it has to be, for neither abstract doctrine nor historical figures nor allegorical personifications are sufficient to explain the nature of the transformation that is offered. Only the combination of history and symbol and myth and personal experience, presented in a form that the mind can take hold of but never exhaust or fully comprehend, will do the job. And that is drama. The talk of the drama of salvation, or salvation history as a play, is not a mere metaphor; it is about as accurate a description as it is possible to give of the way in which the real availability of salvation is made known, and its character explained to human minds.

Within this essentially dramatic awareness, the ritual drama proper has its place: to crystallize and expound the concepts acted out in the drama as a whole. As we saw with the Passover, it can both sum up and energize the inner meaning of the people's whole life. In the same way, the Christian sacraments of Baptism and the Eucharist pull together the themes of the whole drama and present them explicitly. These are tightly knit plays whose words and actions have the same shape as the whole drama and, therefore, make aspects of it both more comprehensible and more powerful in effect. This is because themes normally dispersed in a thousand daily actions and thoughts—such as repentance, unity, exile, hope, or love—are brought together in a thought-out and clear relationship to each other. Thereafter, they are more recognizable *in the salvation context* when they must be developed throughout the overall drama of human birth, love, labor, and death, both individual and racial.

It is noticeable, once one has been alerted to the fact, that a great deal of Scripture commentary has somewhat the character of dramatic criticism. I am not talking here of textual criticism and the research into the historical background of the biblical narratives, but about the vast corpus of reflection on the themes and meanings of Scripture, especially that of the great Fathers of the early centuries. There is a probing into the wider significance of each character, of the relationships between them, and of the actual events. The critic also points out any topical reference, or the way in which the author is challenging the audience to self-criticism or to realize the evils in society to which they have become too accustomed. All this is drawn out by the critic from his consideration of the play; it is not *in* the play in the sense that it is explicit in the text. In the same way, the commentator on Scripture treats the drama of salvation. Among many possible examples, take these extracts from a sermon of Theodotus, Bishop of Ancyra, on the birth of Jesus:

The Lord of all comes in the form of a servant; and he comes as a poor man, so that he will not frighten away those souls he seeks to capture like a huntsman. He is born in an obscure town, deliberately choosing a humble dwelling place. His mother is a simple maiden, not a great lady. And the reason for all this lowly state is so that he may gently ensnare mankind and bring us to salvation. If he had been born amid the splendour of a rich family, unbelievers would surely have said that the face of the world had been changed by the power of wealth. If he had chosen to be born in Rome, the greatest of cities, they would have ascribed the same change to the power of her citizens.

Suppose our Lord had been the son of an Emperor; they would have pointed to the advantage of authority. Imagine his father a legislator; their cry would have been, "See what can be brought about by law." But, in fact, what did he do? He chose nothing but poverty and mean surroundings, everything that was plain and ordinary and, in the eyes of most people, obscure. And this, so that it could be clearly seen that the Godhead alone transformed the world. That is why he chose his mother from among the poor of a very poor country, and became poor himself. . . . See, then, how poverty acted as a prophecy—how his poverty showed that he would become poor for our sake and is thereby made accessible to everyone. . . . he assumed no royal state, which would have driven men away from his presence. No, he came among ordinary men as one of themselves, offering himself freely for the salvation of all mankind.

These ideas are familiar to Christians, but none of them is explicitly stated in the narrative in Luke's Gospel, which is all the text we have for this bit of salvation drama. It is because all those who reflected on it have treated it as a drama, and commented accordingly, that so much which is barely implicit has come to be taken for granted as the proper interpretation of the play. To suggest that the birth of Jesus in a stable and of poor parents was pure bad luck and without significance for his future mission seems ridiculous to us. We can see from this how accustomed we are, without realizing it, to react to the Bible as drama.

In the final example the "critic" makes even clearer that the play contains an implicit demand on the audience, and here the way the actual words of the players are given and commented on makes the drama-criticism nature of this kind of literature even more evident. This is from a sermon of St. Gregory Nazianzen on the Baptism of Christ:

Today Christ experiences baptismal enlightenment; let us also experience it with him. He is baptized; let us go down with him into the waters, so that we may come up from them with him.

As John is baptizing, Jesus presents himself. He comes, perhaps to sanctify the very man baptizing him, certainly to bury the old Adam completely in the waters. In preparation for us and for our sake he hallowed the Jordan, for being himself spirit and flesh he is to baptize with the Spirit and with water.

The Baptist demurs; Jesus contends with him: "It is I who should be baptized by you," says the lantern to the Sun, the voice to the Word, the friend to the Bridegroom, the greatest born of woman to the Firstborn of every creature, he who leaped in his mother's womb to the unborn Child who received his adoration, he who was his forerunner and shall come before him again to the one who revealed himself and shall do so again. . . .

Jesus comes up out of the water, and raises up the whole world with him. He sees the heavens rent open, which Adam had barred for himself and posterity even as Paradise was barred by a flaming sword, and the Spirit coming to meet him, bearing witness to the godhead they both share. The voice comes from heaven, because it is from heaven that he came to whom witness is borne. Taking bodily shape in honour of that body which is itself divine by reason of its union with the divine nature, the Spirit appears as a dove, even as, long ago, we have been told, a dove announced the ending of the flood.

This kind of comment may not appeal to present-day readers, accustomed to a more analytical style, loaded with references to Ugaritic rituals and the iconography of doves. But this "critic" has a splendid grasp of the whole play and, in commenting on this one scene, he refers it to other scenes and to persistent themes in a way that demonstrates both the unity and complexity of the whole, and the several levels—historical, personal, cosmic, communal—on which it is to be understood.

CHAPTER 3

The Role

GOD writes the play; we are all actors, all audiences; but we are all, also, dithering on the edge of the limbo of being neither. If we are to find our place, make the play live, rescue ourselves and our world from nonsense, what is our role to be?

Some time in the early years of the last war a misbegotten experiment was initiated which received some brief publicity. A baby had been adopted by a group of learned and high-minded characters (philosophers, scientists, and educators) whose aim was to rear the infant in total geographical and intellectual isolation from unpleasant influences, in a detached and perfect environment where only good and beautiful ideas and experiences would be available to him

(I think it was "him"). The team had decided to devote their lives and talents to this superchild and, as far as I remember, they hoped the unfortunate infant would therefore live forever, as well as escape the normal ration of suffering. I don't remember the details, only a feeling even then that it wasn't a very realistic project. I have occasionally wondered, since, what happened to that baby. Is he still living in his perfect paradise for one, served by his now very aged guardians, or perhaps younger successors? What is he like, and does he ever get a hint of the horrific realities of life in the outside world in the last thirty-odd years? If he does, what does that do to him? Or did the role thrust on him prove unplayable, and did they let him return to the world, as helpless as a man newly blind?

It seems unlikely that any form of education could so simply cancel out the inheritances of millennia and create what is, in fact, a human being free from original sin—that is, unhampered by the web of offense and defense, of evasion and aggression, by which humans normally both protect and imprison themselves.

But salvation is about just such a transition, and in all the centuries of Christian life and thought and effort the argument has raged over how it is to be accomplished.

The Letter to the Hebrews is interesting here because it concentrates on the role of the Saviour above all, but it interprets that role in terms of earlier models. In much the same way, Shakespeare's great tragic heroes were his own creation, but he took these stories from earlier and cruder tales and developed their significance in undreamed-of ways. The Letter to the Hebrews begins by defining the role of the Son as, among other images, "the perfect copy (rep-

lica) of his (God's) nature." And here at once we have a
dramatic role, because the whole point is that the Son,
made flesh, can only represent the Father by transposing
the glory of the original into a mode that is comprehensible
to those who witness it. Indeed, their witness is the whole
point, and if they were incapable of understanding the
meaning of what they perceived, there would be no saving
effect, no drama, no salvation. So the Son plays the part of
God, to the audience of humankind, and does it as a
human, since that is the only way it can be done.

When we say "plays the part," we immediately feel that
this means a *pretence;* but the reality, as we have seen, is
more complex. His power to "make magic"—which means
the power to play the role convincingly—grows from his
own inner life, and this inner life is that of God himself.
This is the reason that the response, the stir of the magic,
comes from the inner life of the witnesses—the audience.
Their inner life is not glorious; it is not even the raw material of glory; it has not yet been "fused" from the inchoate
elements of fear and hope and nostalgia and excitement and
longing which indicate that there is something to work on.
But it reacts to the performance of the one who consciously
knows the meaning of his own inner life, which can fire the
inner life of the audience and cause that coming together,
that fusion. A new creation of awareness is thus set free to
make the positive personal response whereby actor and audience become one, sharing in that moment the same spirit.

As an analogy, this cannot be pushed too far, but there is,
as pointed out earlier, a sense in which the analogy is also
an example. For the actor who plays a role superbly well is
transformed by it, it both draws on and develops his inner

life. He is not adding something to himself; rather he is giving explicit expression to something in himself which is inherent but, until then, unused and dumb. The limitations of this self-revelation are those of the role he plays and of his own gifts. If we suppose an actor with a uniquely perfect endowment of talent and intelligence, and a role of infinite scope, we begin to get an idea of the effectiveness of Jesus as Christ, and as "radiance of the Father's glory." This is Paul's phrase, clearly the same image as that from the Letter to the Hebrews, just quoted.

It is by the force of the inner life of Jesus, revealed as he plays out his role as Son of God (to use the more familiar image), that salvation is communicated to the audience, moving their own inner life to response and thus to new definition and power. To be saved means, in this context, to be rescued from a sort of spiritual dormancy which might otherwise be permanent, and this by identification with the perfect performance of Jesus as Son, glory, copy of the Father.

We should notice here something which is of fundamental importance in discussing the concept of role-playing in salvation: that the role played by Jesus is that of the player's own self, his fundamental and eternal reality. We shall see later how this works in the traditional Christian spiritual concept of actually taking Jesus as a model and trying to play *him* to the watching world. Here we need to be aware that this fact removes the big difficulty which remains a permanent handicap to the actor of "normal" roles: that wholehearted acting of inevitably one-sided and imperfect characters causes a conflict in the actor's own being. He has to "be" the part, yet he *isn't* the part. And he is not only drained and exhausted by the spiritual tour-de-force involved, he may also be distorted to some extent, perhaps compensating when off-stage by refusing to use the side of his own nature that corresponds to that of the role he plays. (If there were no correspondence at all, he could not release the necessary emotional conviction.)

Many actors develop private affectations which may be partly a defense of the self made too available on stage. Also, the actual employment of emotional power in the role may make the control of similar emotions very difficult in private. If the emotions portrayed are (as they often are) unruly and damaging in their stage effects, they can damage real relationships. The "overflow" emotional life of actors naturally tends to be highly charged. Some learn to cope with this, others seem unable to do so and drift from affair to affair, from jealous scene to jealous scene. On the positive side, stage people are often more responsive than others to "causes," because they have less opportunity to become set in a series of responses built up long before and never touched since. The plight of the needy or the sins of rulers may stir the emotionally active mind of the actor, when other people merely put up their usual shutters of prejudice or laissez-faire policy.

All this makes for an uneasy and dangerous life, because the role exercises only a part of the actor's own personality, thereby unbalancing it. If the role were itself the perfection and totality of the player's own personality (which is impossible in a normal role), it would be developed as a whole, and in balance. The bad effects would not exist, and the good ones (emotional power and sensitivity, strong and insightful reactions to others) would be developed more and more. This is only a shadow of what it means when we think of it happening in Jesus as he plays the role of Son, Word, and radiance of the Father.

But the writer of Hebrews clearly did not find the image of 'copy' explicit enough to explain fully the function of Jesus in the drama of salvation, either in relation to his Father or in relation to those who were to be saved. The role, thus stated, is too all-embracing for the human mind to take hold of. Some way is needed to pin down the type of role the writer is describing, and make it intellectually and imaginatively available. The mystic may enter so far into the mystery that the details of the role are no longer important, but before that stage is reached conversion has to be accomplished, and for that there is a need for some more definable role with which the witness can identify.

T. S. Eliot can say that "the spoken play, the words which we read, are symbols, a shorthand . . . for the acted and felt play, which is always the real thing." But he, who used words with such enormous power, knew very well that the words, apprehended by the intellect, were the only way the "acted and felt play" could get through to the audience. Without words there is no play, the language of mime can take the place of spoken sounds in a limited way, but this becomes simply a substitute form of words, not a way to do without them. Words form the traffic of imagination by which the spirit is moved and enabled to work on the situation as a whole, the movement linking actor and role, role and audience, and audience and actor through the role. And the words have to be concerned with a known and felt experience, one with clear imaginative associations. This will not exhaust the scope of the communication; words are not a definition of the fullness of the role to be played, since a given role extends to the full complexity and unmeasurable spirit of a human being, but they will provide a way in, a gateway of understanding for the audience, which might otherwise be bewildered and repelled by an experience too big to grasp.

This is the function of the famous image of the great High Priest in the Letter to the Hebrews. The writer first states the overall nature of the role of Jesus, who "plays" his Father for the salvation of man, and then provides a way to understand this by means of a symbol of the role—the image of the High Priest—which evokes strong associations for his readers. He strengthens this by referring to Moses, who can also be placed imaginatively by the same symbol, thus making clear that this is a symbol to define the nature of the role, not the role itself. Neither Moses nor Jesus actually functioned as High Priest in the Jewish cult. Yet the symbol enables the witnesses to grasp the nature of the saving work of Jesus. So we might say that the words of the play, as scripted by the author of Hebrews, are about the High Priest, a part played by Jesus. Yet the "acted and felt" play reveals clearly, *through the words*, that the role is much bigger than that.

An example from the real theater may make the distinction clear. J. B. Priestley wrote a play called *An Inspector Calls*. In it, a wealthy Edwardian family, celebrating the daughter's engagement by a family dinner party, is interrupted by a police inspector who has called to conduct an enquiry into the suicide of a pregnant girl who had swallowed a corrosive disinfectant. In the course of questioning the members of the family, the inspector reveals that each of them in some way contributed to the girl's suffering and death. The part of the inspector is written in a style perfectly compatible with that of a police investigator of a certain type—intelligent, patient, stern; not bullying but standing no nonsense; showing compassion as well as occasional outbreaks of anger when confronted with the evasions, smugness, or self-pity of the witnesses.

It gradually becomes clear, however, that he has a wider role in relation to the characters *and to the audience* than merely that of presenting an exciting exercise in detection methods. He is there to stir consciences, to bring sin to light, perhaps to avenge. He exposes the nastiness, weakness, greed, or pathetically wrong values that can lead quite *nice* people to acts of flagrant cruelty. He leaves the family in a welter of mutual recrimination, fear, shame, or defiance, according to character, and the father rings up the police station to check the credentials of the inspector, whose manner he finds suspicious. He discovers that no such inspector is known, and a call to the hospital reveals that no suicide has been admitted that evening. At the exposure of this fraud, the members of the family finally reveal their degree of real repentance, or the reverse. At that moment the telephone rings. A girl, dying of corrosive poisoning, has just been admitted to the hospital. An inspector will be calling to ask a few questions.

In this play the inspector is an inspector and no more, as far as the words that he uses are concerned. But he is more, not merely because the double twist at the end makes this clear, but because of what he does to the other characters all the way through. He is not called God, or Fate, or Conscience, because to tie down the work he does in such a way would be to limit it. His work is bigger than the intellectual content of the role symbol.

The two-leveled role in this play is explicit, but the same thing operates in *all* major dramatic roles. (This does not apply in plays whose purpose is exclusively, or almost exclusively, to entertain intellectually or imaginatively; such as routine farces or thrillers, spectacles or some kinds of drawing-room comedy.) Characters work on each other in ways that extend much further than the scope of their stated roles; for instance, as military leader, nurse, secretary, father, princess, wizard, and so on. This is, of course, equally true of all human interaction, but in drama there is the extra dimension which makes it relevant here—the roles, at both levels, are *public*. That is, they are trying to involve the audience, quite deliberately. The audience are not eavesdroppers; their presence, their reactions, are what it is all about. And part of this is due precisely to their numbers and the fact that audience reaction is a shared experience, one which creates a community of witnesses whose own inner life has, each in his or her own way and degree, been fired into new awareness by the role-playing of the actors.

In the light of this, it is interesting to see how the author of Hebrews uses his symbolic material. The office of a real High Priest is itself, in a sense, dramatic, as is much religious ritual. His role at one point was to represent the whole people in offering sacrifice for sin, and the people saw him do it and identified themselves with what he did. But this, as the writer makes clear, was a one-level role. He could do no more than carry out the explicit rituals for which he was chosen, since he had nothing more to give the people than that. He was, after all, a sinner like themselves; he was on the outside, in a sense, just as much as they were. The actions were not his but God's. He represented the people before God, but not God before the people.

This single level role is not enough, not effective, as the author of Hebrews says. And he emphasizes (Chapter 7) that Jesus was not that kind of priest, either by descent or office. This immediately removes him from the possibility of simply *being* High Priest rather than *playing* it. We have then the possibility (not present in the actual Levitical priesthood) of a two-level role. The kind of High Priest we need, says the writer, is "holy, innocent and uncontaminated, beyond the influence of sinners, and raised up above the heavens"; that is, *over against* the audience, for their own sake, since otherwise he could offer them no more than they know they already have. The raised stage, making the action visible to the whole audience, is the symbol of this need for separation, not in order to separate but to make a closer interaction possible. Yet it is said earlier (4:15) that "It is not as if we had a high priest who was incapable of feeling our weaknesses with us; but we have one who has been tempted in every way that we are, though he is without sin." The one who plays the role must be of the same kind as his audience, so that they can identify with him. But also he is "lifted up" and can set alight the spirit in them by the power of his own inner life as it expresses itself in his performance.

Here we realize something further. The role of High Priest is, according to the writer, played by Jesus when he is triumphant. We can only discern the nature of his whole and fundamental role as the incarnate God when that performance is completed in a way that requires such a symbolic naming in order to make it comprehensible. He has fulfilled the ritual function of the High Priest who passed beyond the veil of the Holy of Holies, but he does it once for all. This capacity to sum up ordinary and frequent human actions, and to give them a dimension and a significance that is both new and permanent, is peculiar to dramatic actions, because they are both common *and* "lifted up," and are able to reveal a significance beyond the level of everyday function. In performance, of course, a play may be repeated hundreds of times, but the significance of the individual role, and of actions within that role, remain "once for all" in the sense that they repeat, for new audiences, the unique significance which it is the dramatic function to evoke.

In the eleventh chapter of the Letter to the Hebrews, the author takes us through the saga of national liberation, with its heroes, the men of faith. But he does not present them as they knew themselves—men with a job to do, more or less under divine guidance but left very much to sort things out as best they could in the ordinary human way. He presents them as men cast for leading roles in a divine drama. He puts them all on the stage in quick succession or in groups, and spotlights them, giving them power and meaning for the reader, as audience. The drama of faith and salvation is presented, but it is clear that, for the real men who did those things in the past, their role was unconscious. They were men of faith, and the dramatic presentation in a sense falsifies the situation as it existed for the people concerned. (The historical status of Abraham, Moses, and others is not the point here, any more than it matters whether the historical Macbeth met witches or the historical Richard III mur-

dered his nephews.) The author knew them as real historical personages, but—like Shakespeare—he used that material for his own purposes. This purpose was to stimulate the
audience to courage in following Jesus.

This is the point. The characters in the Old Testament
drama of salvation were acting parts in a play whose last
act is set on a different plane. Theirs is a play within a play,
and it is only when the audience becomes involved in the
larger drama, which it can watch from outside, that the
denouement becomes possible. This happens when Jesus appears, playing the dual role we have described, and consciously sums up the heroes of faith in his own person. As
the author shows, Jesus in his victory took over the role of
the ritual High Priest and gave it the double level of drama
that converts many, so faith, the catalyst of the event of salvation, finds its perfection as virtue and *as act* in the role of
Jesus as the Suffering Servant. He is, in his own personal
self, both the embodiment of the sufferings of Israel in her
men of faith, and is also, by his human suffering, the means
of involving many in saving and active awareness of the demand of faith, to which they may then freely respond. The
author urges that response, using the obedience and courage of Jesus the man as encouragement. After many warnings against backsliding, he virtually ends the book with
what amounts to a huge transformation scene.

The writing is vividly pictorial, but it is an animated picture with violent and intentionally moving contrasts. It is
not merely descriptive, it is dramatic in the clearest sense,
and it enacts the change from the old Covenant to the new.
It is, perhaps, easier to *feel* this great dramatic climax as a
cinematic rather than a stage one, because of the way the

old and new Covenants are presented in different visual
modes. The author describes the difference by saying that
the new Covenant ("what you have come to") is "nothing
known to the senses," as it was when God made his dramatic points with manifestations of fire or sudden darkness
or raging storms, or the sheer terror of the theophany on
Mount Sinai when even Moses shook with fear. These brief
flash-backs of moments of high intensity in the Jewish experience of the saving but terrible Lord are a complete contrast to what follows. The new Covenant, the manifestation
of what salvation really means now, is presented in equally
visual terms with little abstract language, but there are no
separate scenes, no realism, almost no attempt to arouse
emotion of any kind. Rather, the visual images are perfectly
transparent.

There is a progression as we are moved inwards. "What
you have come to is Mount Zion and the city of the living
God," then we move closer and discover "millions of angels" gathered to celebrate, and with them (but one feels
they are somehow closer to the center) the saved who are all
suddenly "first-born sons" and citizens of heaven. We come
still closer and the author behaves just like a film director,
moving the cameras into close-up and showing us, the audience, that we "have been placed with the spirits of the saints
who have been made perfect" and thus enabled to come
even to God, the Judge, but only because at the heart of it
all is Jesus, the mediator, who brings a new Covenant and
blood for purification. So we discover in ourselves the response to the scene, proving that there is in us that which is
capable of *being* what we are shown, of *becoming* what we experience dramatically.

For this is not an account of the "last things" and the end of the world, it is a dramatic evocation of what is the case *now*, if only we will respond to the performance by the impulse of our own inner life.

"See that you do not refuse him who is speaking," the writer warns. And the "speaker" here is the blood of Jesus spilt in the High Priestly offering, pleading with God. If it was dangerous to refuse the fearful God of the old Covenant, how much worse to reject the "gracious" voice of the new one, which shakes not only earth but heaven—and only what is eternally founded will survive that shaking. The rest will disappear in the "consuming fire."

To refuse to be moved by the drama is to refuse salvation. An elderly French diplomat, with plenty of experience of human corruption in many forms, once said that he thought the most insidiously corrupting thing in his experience was to be moved emotionally and do nothing about it. The person who feels strong emotion over, say, a great film, a real-life tragedy, or a joyful event like a wedding, needs to translate that feeling into some kind of appropriate action such as a conscious effort to be more understanding to others, a gift to a fund to help the needy, or a shift to a more open and hospitable manner of life. The decision can be great or tiny, but it needs to be conscious, and appropriate in some way, and then the emotional experience makes a lasting contribution to the growth of personality. If the feelings are merely allowed to fade out, leaving no more than a faintly nostalgic memory, they are actually corrupting, because they are mere emotional stimulation for its own sake. The traditional concept of emotional catharsis through drama sees the emotional cleansing as a spiritual, converting experience leading to newness of life, at least in some degree. The refusal of this leads to a sort of spiritual hardening, an established resistance to the demands that life makes. Much conventional drama has been designed to cater to this resistance, staying firmly at a noninvolving level, requiring no response but applause for a pleasant escape from reality. Recent drama and dramatists have tried to remedy this, convinced, rightly, that the drama is intended not just to move, but to move to action—the act of faith. Thus the role of the great High Priest, as presented by the author of Hebrews, should move to awe, compassion, joy, and hope, and finally to surrender to the love it enacts.

If action is required, the act of faith requires the follow-up of a faithful life. A conversion is not real unless the enlightenment experienced leads to newness of life, expressed not only in new vision and new attitudes but in a natural development of new patterns of behavior dictated by what has been perceived. And the traditional Christian notion of what kinds of attitude and behavior are involved has always been that of the "imitation of Christ."

This does not mean, and never has meant, an attempt to copy the behavior of the historical Jesus. It means, rather, to be like Jesus in whatever circumstances prevail at the time, and by doing so to change those circumstances as Jesus changed his. In other words, the Christian tries to enact the role of Jesus, a role which must always be presented in the language of the time, place, and personalities involved—in the wide sense of word, gesture, thought.

In one sense, there is only one Christian role—Christ. The Christ whose body is the whole assembly of God's people is the "self," the inner reality of each one. The enact-

ment of the role therefore develops each one in the form of
his *own* personality, without distortion or imbalance. The
Christ role, discovered and studied in the life of the human
Jesus, has a saving significance in the life of the one who
plays it, developing his own eternal self; but it also has, necessarily, a saving function in relation to others, as it had in
the person of Jesus himself. This is at the heart of the theology of the Church, with its great program of education of
those who try to live the Christ-life. The sacraments themselves, symbolizing and reinforcing that life in all its aspects
and stages, make clear the nature of that education and
growth as one of participation in the drama of salvation. In
its very beginning, the rite of Baptism shows the person entering a new life and leaving behind in a symbolic death the
old, sin-limited existence. Its significance is not merely personal but has a dramatic relationship to the whole community involved in it. This applies to all the sacramental acts
of the worshiping community and, indeed, not to the Christian one only. It is a universal religious insight.

But Western Christians, and indeed the whole Western
culture, have difficulty with the idea of infant Baptism, or
with any kind of sacramental ritual; and this is due to the
feeling (more and more powerful since the Renaissance)
that religion is a private and interior affair. If it is purely a
matter of personal response to God's love, pouring water
over a baby (or anyone else, for that matter) seems at worst
a superstitious survival from pagan magic and at best an
outward gesture testifying to an interior act (the really important act) which is already accomplished. But in the Jewish tradition from which Christianity sprang, as well as in
other great religious traditions, this emphasis on the privacy

of religion would seem not so much wrong as meaningless. To Israel, religion was what God did for and to his people, and what he asked of them in return. This meant that each man and woman and child in Israel had a responsibility for the whole people. This responsibility could even be a frightening one, for the failure of one might bring disaster on all. But each one discovered and kept (or broke) God's covenant with the whole people. It is by involving oneself wholeheartedly in the covenant relationship between God and his people that an individual can achieve holiness, and be marked out, perhaps, for a special mission. The drama was played out by a whole people.

Given this strong and basic sense of a people's bond with the saving God, it was natural that the stages and crises of family, national, and agricultural life should be marked and celebrated with public ritual. The Jewish boy was circumcized at eight days, and although the date depended on his birthdate—not on a national or religious calendar—it was a public act, signifying his incorporation among the chosen people. The later *bar mitzvah,* the coming of age at thirteen, was and is a personal and family affair, but it makes no sense apart from the religious identity of the whole people of Israel. By it, the boy on the verge of adulthood consciously takes on his ritual and moral responsibility as an adult male in Israel, the nation of priests. He takes on the role of mediator, one of those charged with keeping and teaching the Covenant, maintaining in good order Jacob's ladder from earth to heaven.

Both of these Jewish ceremonies lend something to the understanding of Baptism, by which a person takes on a role that is his own personal one and on which his own selfhood depends. It is at the same time a role in relation to the community at large, and *with* the community, which also has a saving role in relation to the unconverted world.

The Eucharist is an action whose importance in the understanding of Christian role-playing is central. Here the individual eats and drinks with others in a sacred meal which makes them one, as Paul says. This "one" is Christ, who is present as Saviour for each one. And insofar as the saving effect really works in each one, they are the more made into one body and able to act as Christ—Saviour—to the world. This rite means a great deal to people trying to follow, or act, Christ at many different levels. The two-way movement of this play-within-a-play is inward and then outward. The people come to God in and by Jesus, offering him as he offered himself, but symbolically, in a way that clearly shows that *they* are part of the offering and share in the roles of sacrifice—victim and priest. This opening up to God, perfectly shown in the death and rising of Jesus, makes it possible to identify more completely with the whole Christ-role. The receiving of the consecrated food, now made a material sign of the role of the community, reinforces that role, making clear the Christ-role, not just of the whole but of each member.

The paradoxical but experientially accurate assertion of Paul—"I live, yet now not I, but Christ lives in me"—here finds its expression in terms of physical gesture, symbol, and psychological experience all at once; though, of course, the degree of awareness can vary from nil to near-total. This central experience, attested in other terms by all genuine religious traditions and modes, is less baffling when considered in terms of dramatic role-playing. The "I" here, shifts in meaning between the first and second use of the word. The first "I" is the essential self, the total, eternal, yet individual human person which indwells, animates, and also really *is* the being of the exterior, perceptible personality. The second, exterior, "I" can be called the "ego" or "persona" or any other of the various words used to express this difficult concept. It is not, in any case, clearly circumscribed, and various categorizations overlap. It is the region of the person which is involved in the messy condition summed up as "sin." But this exterior personality, the one we are normally aware of and have to deal with in ourselves and others, is to be finally dissolved into the essential "I," the Self or Spirit. In this it does not lose definition or simply fade out, but rather it discovers its reality as the limiting factors are overcome.

This exterior "persona" is a mask, which is what the word means, and indeed many masks may be tried on before one is found that begins to correspond to the truth of personality and makes possible the growth of the true Self. Many people take on a mask that suits the circumstances and satisfies others, and they cling to this and cultivate it as their real self. Thus they may "act a part" in the wrong sense of simply going through the motions of a personality that is unreal, finally. Edith Evans, as quoted by Michael Redgrave in his book *Mask or Face*,* once remarked with a certain gentle irony, "I envy some of you young people who seem to start off your careers at the very outset with a personality of your own. It took me years to find mine, peeling off layer after layer of myself like an onion until I found the

* Michael Redgrave, *Mask or Face*. Heinemann, London, England. 1958.

essence." Many people never even realize that they have not found the essence. The fake personality that the insecure young adopt so firmly is a barrier to that "stripping" which is a prelude to true and deep role-playing, the transforming one.

It is this transformation which is signified by the word Christ, referring to the Person or Self in whom all persons find their own Self and identity. This discovery comes about by playing the part assigned to one by Baptism—that of Christ—and gradually entering more and more into the role, which corresponds in its outward behavior patterns to the needs of the real Self. In this way, it creates a unity between the Self "I" and the outward "I." So it comes about that it can be true for Paul to say *both* that "I" live—the whole self—and that it is *not* "I" but Christ who lives in me, because the Christ role is now "myself."

Within this development of the whole community and its members, there is a need for role-playing of a different kind. The organization of the outward nature—the "flesh" of Pauline theology—demands differentiation of community functions for its continued and satisfactory daily life. We are still "babes in Christ," inexpert actors requiring tuition and—above all—experience. There are different temporal roles in the business of training the "players" of salvation. But these, important as they are, only serve the central purpose of transformation of each person and of the whole community of man and earth, in Christ. Technique comes in here, and is essential and valuable.

At this point it is helpful to spend some time looking at the place of technique and the idea of education, authority, tradition, and so on, in Christian life, before going on to consider eschatology in the dramatic categories already explored.

Paul, not thinking in dramatic categories (except unintentionally, which is revealing), used the metaphor of a normal kind of education to explain the status and needs of the human race. He compared it to the position of the heir to a great estate who is still too young to inherit and has to have guardians or trustees.

I mean that the heir, as long as he is a child, is no better than a slave, though he is the owner of all the estate; but he is under guardians and trustees until the date set by his father (Galatians 4:1, 2).

There is an interesting implication here, not spelled out but clear, that this "heir"—the human race itself—is orphaned, or at least his Father is away on a very long journey. God is not, in fact, absent from his people, but being, as we saw, isolated and ignorant through sin, fearful and beset by the unknown, they feel as if he is. In this orphaned condition man does not even know that he is the heir, and the trustees and guardians have the job of preparing him for that knowledge, and for entering the inheritance when the time comes. They are not always either very conscientious or very intelligent, but they do the job somehow.

If we elaborate the image a little, as Paul does not, we can get quite a lot of help from it.

It is clear that a lot depends on the kind of education given to the heir of great estates before he comes into his own. If his Father is present, and they have a close relationship, there is no problem. The heir learns, through love and respect and emulation, to be exactly the kind of person to fit the inheritance. (Here is the place of role-playing as we have seen it.) We can also see here, perhaps, the reason why Christ is the Son, the first-born and natural heir who, as we saw, "plays the Father" for mankind. But if the Father is away or dead, then everything depends on those tutors and custodians. Paul would say, presumably, that the Jewish law, the magnificent Torah revealed to Moses, was the best possible tutor. "The law was our custodian until Christ," and if it was a harsh guardian it was an efficient one; it kept the inheritance intact, if un-enjoyed, and provided an ethical training that made (or should have made) the people ready to recognize the time of their inheritance. It prepared, as it were, an audience with sufficient sensibility to understand the play.

There are other tutors, for every culture and tribe has had and still has its own "law," which fulfils its proper purpose when it helps people to grow up spiritually to the point where they are able to assume their own destiny in freedom. Manifestly, most kinds of law do not do this. On the contrary, the "tutors" strive to possess people, body and soul, in a state of permanent enslavement to custom and law and the mental patterns laid down by tradition. The drama of salvation itself may be interpreted by them so as to nullify the actual experience of salvation.

Now Paul was thinking chiefly of the turning point in history at which the Christ appeared. This moment is the announcement that "we are no longer under a custodian, for in Christ Jesus you are all sons of God, through faith." And he constantly pushed and persuaded and shoved and exhorted his converts to live up to that, to become *really* the free men they were invited to be, acting the role of the free Christ: "not I, but Christ in me." To what extent he realized that the custodial process had to go on, even though Christ had come, it is hard to say. It seems that he did not fully work it out in theory, but he knew it in practice, from the sheer hard work he had to do with his constantly backsliding Christians. But whether he knew it or not, it is clear to us that the coming of Christ was not only once for all to mankind, but was also for each man and woman, as each reaches the point at which one can cry "Abba! Father" through the power of the spirit, responding, in the Christ-role, to the Father whose image Christ is.

And in practice the chief work of the Christian Church has been (even in Paul's day) to provide the tutorial system which should prepare people to recognize and accept the inheritance of Christ, as well as to sustain and nourish those who have already received it. The function of the community of believers is to *prepare* people for salvation, to guide toward full freedom the personality which has been enlightened, as well as to try to lead it to initial enlightenment. We find ourselves back at the question of Baptism, and especially infant Baptism. It is connected closely with the struggle in the contemporary theater to find a true personalism, a total spontaneity, and with this goes a deep suspicion of learned technique and traditional methods and ideas. In the same way, at present, the custodial function of the Christian community and its relation to salvation is one of the touchiest theological issues. The past overemphasis on hierarchical structure and clerical authority in most Christian Churches has made people, accustomed to secular democratic ideals, extremely suspicious of any ideas that smell of paternalism, just as actors and directors dislike over-direction. The recovered emphasis on personal commitment and personal responsibility appeals to this mentality, and with it goes the popularity of situation ethics, in which the individual, in a sense, creates morality by personal efforts at love and truthfulness as the occasion requires, just as the ideal modern actor creates his role. Sin means the failure to judge and act lovingly.

The idea that there might be a wrong-ness that requires no deliberate act of involvement, yet is of itself damaging to the human being touched by it, is unacceptable to many modern Christians. The ideal is the autonomous, mature human being, responsible for his or her actions before God. Such a person may make a free and conscious choice, and commit himself or herself to Christ by being Baptized, and this is regarded as fitting and meaningful. Having made such a choice, a nurturing and teaching Church is not necessary, though the companionship and moral support of the Church, in the sense of a community of believers, is good and desirable. The parallel with the groups of actors, who, ideally, would do without a director altogether, is clear.

This idea appears at first sight unexceptionable and right, for Christ is the ideal and he is the one with the fullness of grace, consciously taking on the role of his Father, freely accepting all that it entails, and free to judge and act as seems best to him as his Father's son. But while the Christ may serve as an ideal, the man Jesus does not exactly fit the requirements made of one who has no need of tutelage. The essential freedom of his role seems to have been something whose nature and purpose Jesus *discovered*, over a period, and there are signs of this discovery going on. For instance,

in the story of the woman who was healed without his conscious knowledge or consent by touching his clothes; and in
that of the Syro-Phoenician woman, where what appears to
be a genuine uncertainty about the scope of his mission was
resolved in a curious interchange whose meaning was
clearly more in the personal challenge and response than in
the actual words. And at all times Jesus obeyed the Torah,
though he did not always regard the interpretation of it by
contemporary moralists as necessarily equally important.

In trying to understand the spiritual and psychological
development of Jesus, there are obvious exegetical pitfalls,
and one can easily read too much into records made for
purposes (and with topical allusions) about which we are
not fully informed and probably never will be. We are on
much firmer ground if we turn to Paul's letters and see the
kind of problems he had to deal with among the believers in
the new faith, and the way his own thinking evolved in con-
sequence. One of the most frequently recurring problems is
that of the contrast between the status of spiritual men,
which is proper to those liberated by faith, and the kinds of
behavior, anxieties, and priorities manifested in practice by
so many converts. Paul is constantly exhorting his converts
to behave like free men, to stop worrying about regulations
and factions, to treat each other as befits people who have
died and risen to new life. As actors, they must not rely on
technical tricks but play the Christ-role from the heart. On
the one hand he is moved by their faith and goodness:

We know, brothers, that God loves you and that you have been
chosen, because when we brought the Good News to you, it came
to you not only in word, but as power and in the Holy Spirit and
as utter conviction (1 Thessalonians 1:4).

He also wrote to the Church in Thessalonica: "This has made you the great example to all believers. . . . you are our pride and joy."

Yet even his beloved Thessalonians—the least of his problems and the greatest of his joys among the Churches he founded—needed to be reminded to avoid fornication, and not to worry about the fate of those who died. They still needed, in fact, both moral and doctrinal instruction, and it seems there were those among them charged with giving just this. Their position, it seems, was sufficiently delicate for a gentle reminder about them to be necessary: "We appeal to you, my brothers, to be considerate to those who are working amongst you and are above you in the Lord as your teachers." These may have been traveling apostles, but it sounds more as if they were local people with a permanent responsibility. Evidently, even the best of converts still needed guidance.

And to other Churches Paul had occasion to be much fiercer, denouncing behavior which was very much "of the flesh," as he himself points out. "You are still unspiritual," he tells the Corinthians. "Isn't that obvious from all the jealousy and wrangling that there is among you, from the way you go on behaving like ordinary people?" In this connection, a quotation from Stanislavski is interesting:

The worst stumbling block in an actor's work is that dreadful habit of mind which always seizes on a man's bad points and his most glaring faults. . . . That is why their own stage images are so one-sided and false.*

* Constantin Stanislavski, *Stanislavski on the Art of the Stage.* David Magarshack, tr. Hill & Wang, Inc., New York, 1962; Faber & Faber Ltd.

The quarrelsome, critical behavior that Paul had occasion to point out so many times is liable to make people cling to their masks, the "one-sided and false" images, either as a defense against criticism or as the means for justifying criticism of others. The false character so assumed has a life of its own and can play the role of "righteous anger" or "martyred innocence" quite easily. It is only by abandoning such behavior that the mask can safely be set aside, and the true spiritual role undertaken. It is not easy, as Stanislavski says:

The switching over of your inward attention, though difficult at first, gradually becomes normal. What is normal becomes, not at once but again gradually, easy, and finally what is easy becomes beautiful. It is only then that *the beautiful in yourself* begins to evoke corresponding vibrations of the beautiful in every man. . . . Without such a thoroughgoing and voluntary self-preparation it is impossible to become an actor—the reflection of the treasures of the human mind.

My italics, for *the beautiful in yourself* is the true role which corresponds to the reality of the self. And the long and difficult effort at self-preparation clearly requires guidance, support, and encouragement—such as that given to young actors by Stanislavski himself. This corresponds to Paul's conclusions about his converts. Since they still behaved in the unspiritual ways he had described, they still needed to be guided and admonished. For this purpose there were "guardians in Christ," though Paul contrasts these with himself who, as their first evangelist, begot them "in Christ Jesus" and was their "father." In either case, a continuing tutelage is implied.

To the Galatians—even more of a problem, though for different reasons—he refers to himself as a "mother," and compares the process of evangelizing to that of giving birth, evidently a difficult birth, too. But the image carries its unstated corollary: if to evangelize is to give birth, then it is not the end of the process but very nearly the beginning, and there are many years of work and effort and anxiety and passionate carefulness still ahead before "Christ is formed in you." So, indeed, Paul found it, and so has every Christian teacher and preacher ever since, laboring to coach novice actors in the salvation drama.

The aberrations of overemphasis on law, and on authority, are many and glaring and disastrous, but it is impossible to do without these things. They have constantly to be rethought in relation to their purpose, which is to assist and support the clumsy and nervous efforts of the "babes in Christ." This does not mean that there is a time in human growth when tutelage must cease. The problem is more difficult than that, because all through life, from cradle to deathbed, there is an element of true self-ness, and also an element of falsity. The proportions vary but the two are always there. And the support required is not merely moral but also intellectual, because the nice Victorian idea that one can behave in a morally acceptable way whatever one's ideas about the nature of people, life, and death, has been all too obviously exploded. Belief affects conduct, though not necessarily at once, because learned moral customs can carry people on for a long time after the doctrinal underpinning of the customs has rotted away. In the end, however, they collapse, and so do the moral habits of, for instance, respect for innocent life or marital fidelity.

On the other hand, thinking of the concepts of authority, tradition, training, and so on, in terms of salvation drama helps to de-fuse the defensive feelings that these arouse, not only by giving a different approach but because they make better sense that way. Actors, however talented, find the need for a director if their own work is to be done in the best way, and they rely on learned techniques, and on all the games and exercises of their training, to use body, voice, and mind to the best advantage. On the other hand, the good director tries to be, as far as possible, unnecessary. He may have to correct, to repeat and repeat scenes, even to rethink a whole production halfway through. He may be fierce and cause arguments and rows, but his aim is not to make the actors present *his* production, but to work *with* them to present the play well. If he truly does this, his cast will accept his criticisms and patiently endure his temperament, knowing it is not mere self-interest. The comparison with the relation between guides and pupils in the spiritual life does not need to be labored, provided one remembers that in the spiritual life a person may be at one time chiefly actor and at another chiefly director, and always, in any case, a bit of both.

CHAPTER 4

Actors, Audience and Language

O NE characteristic of the Passover festival in its present form—that is, since the destruction of the Temple— is that it is a family ritual. In the Temple period the killing of the Passover lamb was carried out in the Temple by adult males only, with careful purity rituals. (They were not priests, however. This was the one sacrifice not offered by the Levitical priesthood but by ordinary family men.) But after a while it became customary for wives and families to come to Jerusalem and share in the meal itself, which is now called the Seder in the Western Jewish tradition. There are family and household rituals in most religious traditions, but they are normally domestic in character. They elaborate family occasions such as weddings or funerals, ask blessings on the household itself, or are part of the regular religious practice of individuals worshiping as a group. There are also local festivals and rituals and—at one time— gods.

The Seder is unique in being definitely a national festival concerned with the whole people worshiping one God according to a single ritual celebrated simultaneously by all. Yet, since the destruction of the Temple it is celebrated only in households, whether they be families or groups of people such as in a school or kibbutz. This means that only a comparatively small number of people are present together for the feast, and it is because of this characteristic that something else emerges—in this play there is no audience, all are actors.

Those who take part in the Seder ritual are all Jews, with perhaps an occasional guest. There are different roles for father, mother, youngest child, various readers, but even those who are not playing leading roles are all part of the cast, joining in songs and prayer and above all in the very action of sharing this meal which is also the drama of a people's salvation. There is no distinction between clergy and congregation, all are "priests," according to the word of the Lord to Israel through the mouth of Moses: "I will count you a kingdom of priests, a consecrated nation."

The sense of this is that every member of God's people is to be regarded as having an explicit role in the drama of salvation. The whole people is to carry out the Lord's will, not merely a chosen group, even though the sons of Levi have priestly functions of sacrifice which others normally do not. What makes a priest a consecrated person in this context is not a specific ritual qualification but membership of a people saved from slavery for God's purposes, and well aware of it.

In one sense, then, if "audience" means a group whose conscious purpose is not only to watch but to react and to be somehow caught up in the action at least interiorly, this drama of salvation has no audience. But the prophets and the chroniclers and poets of the nation had a clear sense that there was an "unintentional" audience, an audience of Gentile nations who would be impressed, enraged, or frightened, even against their will, by the way God cared for his people. It was this sense of being the center of God's salvific action, the ones used to carry out the divine purpose among the nations, that made it so difficult to accept defeat and exile and the apparent destruction of the whole people as a people. Yet it was this catastrophic event which, in the end, created the special Jewish spirituality, the conviction of a vocation which is more than mere nationalism but has a mystical sense which makes nationhood all the stronger and deeper.

It was during the period of exile that the synagogue developed, a meeting place for prayer and study in order to preserve the faith and traditions and learn to understand the continuing reality of Yahweh's love even in exile. So, though the Passover ritual and the synagogue worship has no clergy, in these ways the whole nation is being steadily taught to become God's "players," consciously enacting the drama of salvation through the covenant relationship with God before all nations.

This idea of an exterior audience is quite secondary in practice, however. It lies at the back of the mind, the front is occupied with the enactment itself and what it does to those who take part. The priest-less nature of the period of Jewish history after the destruction of the Temple (and in a lesser degree between the exile and the rebuilding) creates an important difference between the Judaic religious sense and that of those religions of which a specially priestly group, with specific and exclusive sacred functions, is an essential part. The Islamic tradition shared this priest-less nature, and so did Christianity at first, though both drifted into a tacit acceptance of differentiation between the priests (teachers or officially trained leaders) and the ordinary mass of believers who were, on the whole, expected to watch and listen and respond—to be audience, not players.

This drift, and the acceptance, by religions like Hinduism and the ancient cults of the Near East, of a priestly elite as the inevitable and proper social structure of religion, needs to be looked at carefully. It seems clear that to dispense with a sacred class, whose job is to perform sacred functions for the rest, goes against the grain of human nature as it normally works.

It is often said that only a war can get people to cooperate across all lines of class, religion, or whatever other social divisions are accepted in a particular society. It is true that war does this, because the motive of defeating the enemy or resisting him overrides other considerations. The same thing happens in many kinds of emergency situations, and once the emergency is over things return to "normal." A now dated, but still perceptive play, *The Admirable Crichton*, was a study of exactly how this happens. An aristocratic household is shipwrecked on a desert island, and Crichton, the butler, an intelligent and resourceful man, is freed by the circumstances from the inevitable subservience to which his class origins had confined him while they remained in England. Crichton becomes the leader, and his former employers soon accept the position and their practical inferiority. He is about to marry the daughter of the family, previously engaged to a nice aristocratic nitwit, when a rescue ship arrives. The butler, still using the intelligence that gave him his ascendancy, realizes that going back to England means going back to the old pattern of master/servant relationship. The others are embarrassed at first, but quickly adjust both their behavior and their memories of the reversal of roles during their island interlude.

This is very much what happened to Christianity. The Jewish religious sense had already been given a taste of emergency conditions in the exile, and from this, as we have seen, grew the synagogue and the greater reliance on the family as the religious center. The Temple cult, though vital, was no longer absolutely essential, but in a sense this was a return to a more primitive awareness, when a small, poor, embattled nation, faced with the power of a large, highly civilized one, had found its sole strength in *each* man's assurance of being one of the Chosen. The Roman occupation, as such things do, sharpened distinctions. Some Jews dealt with the situation as a political one in which the old faith was a powerful tool, while others found in it the stimulus to a deeper and more demanding spirituality, as the Pharisees had done in the Maccabean period. From the time of the siege of Jerusalem, Jewish religion has been always in an emergency situation, so that the sense of religious identity overrode all other differences, and this identity was fostered and strengthened in every possible way by ritual, education and life-style. All the people were the players of the salvation drama, and early Christianity adopted this view and strengthened it in spite of—or even because of—a strong missionary sense.

The first Christians grew spiritually from the emergency situation of a whole people, having their own inner and traditional security of custom and history to sustain them. But they emerged into a more precarious situation, in which the security was wholly spiritual, God-derived, since it was soon rejected by the bulk of the Jewish people and had not made more than a handful of Gentile converts. These first churches were in every way in an emergency situation. Each member severally had given up a previous religious context and the support it offered; and each, by doing so, easily put at risk family approval and job security. In the case of slaves they risked punishment and even death. Death soon became a familiar risk for all the churches. Added to this, the churches were in constant expectation of the ending of all things, though it is arguable that this was more the effect than the cause of their exposed and insecure situation. Whether cause or effect, it was part of their general sense of the contingency of life. In this situation their sense of being God's picked players was intense. They were the ones chosen to enact the drama of salvation before all the world, and the world's gaze was much more part of their daily awareness than it was for the Jews. They bore witness effectively to a conscious part of the Christian calling, and this was to be done not only by example, as Paul recommended, but by preaching and teaching, in public and private, "in season and out of season," no matter what the consequences.

The new churches were, and knew they were, players, not

audiences. But they were not a professional elite within a mass of regular theatergoers, as were religions with a permanent, priestly, sacred area. Their aim was to change the audience to actors, if they could, or at the very least to reveal by their playing the nature of good and evil and so to make choices plain. For this to happen, there has to be a latent desire for it in the audience, an uneasiness, a disillusion with existing structures and beliefs. Their situation is, then, exactly the opposite of that which has created the regular theater audiences of the West in the recent past (and cinema audiences, too) as well as the regular churchgoers or templegoers of past and present. These audiences attend the performance on the understanding that they are to remain detached, though they expect to be moved, perhaps purified, and enabled to understand themselves better. They come to take part in the celebration of traditional and accepted values, whether social or religious, or possibly to be moved to consider reforming them for the better, but never to question them fundamentally.

Peter Brook, discussing the search for a way to reach new audiences, now that the old ones are dwindling, sees the new actors as necessarily "out of tune with society, not seeking to celebrate the accepted values but to challenge them." There is already an awareness of a need for change, a restlessness that is not satisfied with the available forms, and it is in such a situation that the other kind of players, such as those new, crude little churches of the apostolic era, can work effectively. To quote Peter Brook once more:

Were new phenomena to come into being in front of an audience, and were the audience open to them, a powerful confrontation would occur. Were this to occur, the scattered nature of social thinking would gather round certain bass notes; certain deep aims would be refelt, renewed, reasserted. In this way the divisions between positive and negative experience, between optimism and pessimism, would become meaningless.

Mixed metaphors apart, this is a useful statement of what happened in response to the existence and preaching of the apostolic Church. The new teaching caused basic human aspirations to be felt anew, and this was possible because these ancient desires were given a totally new form, one that gave them a completeness of articulation, a hope, and a dynamism that had not been possible before. This is what the salvation drama is for, and it was effectively played by the new churches because they were a dedicated group in which the whole of life was integrated—painfully and publicly, but persistently—into one hope and love. That hope and love was able to express itself to others through these actors, and to become vividly perceptible to their audience. In such a situation as theirs, there was no place for smugness, or reliance on tradition without the inner vitality of personal discovery.

There is a strangely (or perhaps not so strangely) Pauline echo about the following passage from Stanislavski in which he urges (yet again) self-criticism and the eradication of pride and egoism and false confidence. In his method of training, he was trying to create a group of actors who could reach hearts, move, transform. And his desire always escaped his achievement, because the aim that drove him, and his pupils through him, could not be satisfied with what the commercial theater, however great, can compass, though it may touch it at moments. He says:

There were unhappy periods in the history of the theatre during which living art ceased to exist, being replaced by dry-as-dust, dead form. But it revived once more as soon as artists appeared whose taste for life in art brought their love to a state of entirely selfless loyalty to it, to a point when they were ready to give up their greatest treasure of heart and soul to the service of art. In my system, according to which I am conducting my work with you, I am always trying to rouse your enthusiasm for the examination of the nature of your own creative powers. I want to eradicate all your hackneyed stage conventions and replace them by new principles of creative art which prevent the actor from getting into a groove. . . . May you always be clad in cloaks made of scintillating, genuine feelings and thoughts. By this you will not only force the spectator to follow everything that is taking place on the stage, but there will also be in all your songs the true expression of thought—word—sound, and then I, with the rest of the spectators, will say, "I believe in you."

"I believe in you." That is the aim, for this kind of playing changes people who watch it so that they become moved to an act of faith, of willed involvement, or at least it challenges them to choose whether or not they will respond. Many refuse, and return thankfully to noninvolving drama, expert but well separated from the issues of actual living— what Peter Brook calls "deadly theatre." Paul would have used the same word, I think. The aim of salvation drama, lived and spoken, is to transform in faith, and the repetition of old formulae of faith will not do that. Only vivid, personal self-giving to the enactment of God's play will do that.

But the fact is that most people, even when belief is sincere, can't live for long at the ptich of effort demanded by Stanislavski—and Paul. This is why the big religious tradi-

tions, embracing whole populations in the scope of a system
which is cultural as much as religious, always have a division between those whose special vocation is to enact the
drama of salvation in some sense, and those who, while be-
lieving, have no permanent sacred function. At intervals
they *participate* in the sacred, like an audience in a theater,
but then they go home, refreshed and encouraged, to cope
with the necessities of daily life.

In the not-very-long run, Christianity also fell into this
pattern and has remained in it ever since the first century,
but it did not do so comfortably, as did Hinduism or the
small cults that depend on the inspiration and esoteric gifts
of particularly chosen individuals. Christianity had the
wrong sort of theology to be comfortable with this division,
since the whole trend of the Gospel message, in its Jewish
roots and its Pauline exposition, was a call to become a
community of the transformed, with distinction of function
but not of status, as between "sacred" minister and "pro-
fane" laity. As we have seen this had led, whenever conditions encouraged it, to those recurrent attempts to recapture
the total Gospel community, in which all believers are actors and the audience is the outside world, the not yet converted, consisting of potential new actors.

A religious culture with a secure socioeconomic background such as that of the nineteenth century middle
classes, will be comfortable with the sacred-profane separation; and its missionary efforts, if any, will be thought of as
entirely exterior—a touring company, taking culture to pro-
vincial backwaters. Only when its fundamental tenets are
undermined by events (personal or public) will it be open to

becoming the other kind of audience, the kind that is open to challenge.

The trouble is that though the conditions are favorable—the psychological and spiritual shake-up of a whole culture can seldom have been more thorough than it is now in the West—people have seen the Christian play before, or at least they think they have—which comes to the same thing, since in either case they will stay away.

This helps us to understand the lengths to which some Christians go to create a new "theatrical experience" and thus reach a new and hitherto resistant audience. It nearly always seems to mean trying new liturgical forms, whether prearranged or essentially and startlingly spontaneous, but this shows a fundamental misconception about the relation between actors and audience, the same one which now bedevils the actual theater. For the attempts to lure uninterested people into the theater and make them into an audience, assumes an essential separation between players and spectators. There may be talent among the spectators, some may emerge and join the troupe, but an audience is an audience and has no essential function beyond that of appreciation (and paying for seats). But that kind of audience, as we have seen, only exists in a culture with settled values, which requires a theater (or a religion) merely to celebrate and confirm or "constructively criticize" what everyone knows. There is scope for shocking such an audience a little, giving them a pleasantly guilty thrill, as Shaw and other social-comment dramatists did. But such drama does not transform people and is not expected to. It can fill houses, and that is what makes it a "success," which is the criterion now being applied to religious behavior, in or out of churches. Does it attract the crowds? Are people impressed? Do they support us, come to church, admire our campaigns?

But the criterion of the success of salvation drama is not whether it fills houses but whether it *saves*. This doesn't necessarily mean counting how many people actively join the group of players; it does mean realizing that the distinction between audience and actors is accidental, not essential. The line of salvation is not drawn at the footlights, it is drawn (but only God can see it) in a wavering and ever-changing contour between those who respond, are open and changing, and those who watch unmoved, or moved by the pleasure of the emotion, with no aftereffect but a pleasant exhilaration of the mind and feelings.

The essential message of the Gospel in this respect is exactly that. The drama of salvation is played not only *to* all men and women but, if only they will respond, *by* them. The explicit roles are recognizable; not all can play leads, not all even appear on the stage or operate behind the scenes. There are those who are temperamentally and circumstantially audience, in the sense that their share in the production is the essential one of assisting at it. They give themselves to the play, evoke and almost create the power and meaning which is latent in the words and actions of the players. Every actor and director knows the difference a good audience makes. A good audience can take a difficult play, one with elusive meanings and many layers of significance, and make the thing suddenly come clear *to the actors*. The excitement of such an experience is something unforgettable. It cannot be held, preserved, or repeated, but it becomes part of the basic understanding of the play from that time forward. In the context of salvation, the analysis of such an experience so that its lessons—though not of course itself—may be preserved is what theology is about, and has to do with the meaning of tradition when it is a living thing.

How this happens in the theater is recognized, though not frequently—peak experiences seldom are. It is important to recognize the same thing in the development of salvation drama. A tiny example from personal experience may illustrate this. A young couple were to be married, and although their Christian beliefs were off-beat and uncertain they were sincere, and sincere in their notion that a marriage had meaning. Their friends were mostly of similarly hazy religious affiliations, some had none, a few were explicitly Christian. There were also present many relations and friends of an older generation, of different denominations but respectably Christian. This was reflected in the dress of the congregation which ranged from patched jeans and Afro hair styles to dinner jackets. The music was provided by a group of young friends with guitars, and was "folk" but, out of deference to the older generation, not very far out. And the ritual was the normal one of marriage and nuptial Eucharist. It should, according to expectation, have been a pleasant, touching occasion with something for everyone. Something happened to it, and it became much more. This was partly due to the attitude of the officiating priest, who was in tune with the feelings of the unbelieving or half-believing young who wondered if they were being hypocritical by attending such a ceremony.

By stressing the way in which coming to celebrate a marriage is an act of love and actually makes it, he gave them a role they could accept. Some barriers went down. The music—nostalgic and disturbing and not especially religious in the usual sense—did something to break down a few more. The unashamed presence of the young couple's baby, born four months earlier, perhaps helped also to strip away a few layers of pretense.

How can one define exactly why, at a certain moment, old words begin to mean something new and regulation gestures become almost frighteningly significant? All one can say is that, somehow, the spiritual temperature rose. The old play was suddenly a new play, the joining of one man and one woman, seen dozens of times—a cliche, a bad joke, a pious hope—became vital, moving, an act involving all present in ways none could define but all (as it emerged afterwards) felt in some way or other.

The moment came for the distribution of Holy Communion, first to the bride and groom, as expected, and then to those in the congregation who were members of that church, as expected. Only, somehow, the expected didn't happen, for as the little groups of church "regulars" approached the altar steps, there was a kind of rustle and wavering in the back rows, and, hesitantly, a young man in jeans clambered out of his bench and joined the line. Then another followed him, and a girl. Then an older man, a member of another church, rose, and then several more, then more young ones. It was impossible to tell which were Christians, or half Christians, or nonbelievers, or merely nonthinkers. For that moment, all were believers in the transforming significance of what was being done, of this coming together of a man and a woman, and of others with them, sharing the symbolic meal that signified precisely that sharing, that celebration. It was sheer chance that the musicians, coming to the end of the song chosen to accompany the Communion, flicked through their books for another to fill the time as the line before the altar grew longer and longer, and came up with "O Sinner Man." After that there was a silence, but a silence that shimmered with an unexplainable, fragile, already retreating sense of rightness and fulfillment. Actors and audience were one. Who was actor? Who was audience? The distinction vanished for the time, yet the explicit roles were never in doubt.

Examples of this on a larger scale or a more historic occasion might be described, but the unimportant small-scale occurrence is significant becuase it shows how the Gospel notion about the oneness of a transformed people is not a mere projection of unearthly hope, or the prerogative of a very fervent minority, but is an everyday possibility for anyone. In this case, the degree in which this experience becomes decisive, or even very memorable, depends on all kinds of personal factors, but the thing happens, all the same. For the time, there is an experience of oneness, a special kind of oneness which is more than unity of purpose, as at a political rally, or the mental affinity in a group of old friends or a happy family.

The special kind of oneness comes from participation in an experience to which all contribute yet which is bigger than any or all, and not within their power to create or define, singly or collectively. It is a real transformation, at least for the time. People find themselves on the brink of knowing something in themselves that isn't normally available, and this happens as part of an essentially collective experience in which definite roles can be discerned, yet which is clearly not initiated or controlled by even the most important role-player. The quietest, least demonstrative member of the audience may be contributing as much to the total discovery as the leading actor or the director.

There is a good deal more to the audience-actor relationship, however, than being willing to be caught up in one of those intense moments when the drama of salvation becomes the definitive ingredient in human experience, illuminating and coordinating all the rest. There are the other days, the other levels. There are the times when audiences dwindle, when, at least for a time, only those with a definite role to play can keep the troupe going, as in a diaspora situation, where there is no audience to make a big, mixed, dramatic community. Only the experienced actors and their students, convinced of the value of the drama, continue patiently rehearsing, keeping the tradition alive in attics and hired rooms, rejected and hated by respectable theatergoers.

For hundreds of years the Jewish people kept their play in rehearsal, sometimes in strangely garbled versions, repeating foreign words learned by rote, and gestures whose meaning was forgotten. The Spanish Jews, descended from forcibly converted ancestors, long out of touch with any real Jewish life, doggedly repeated what they could only vaguely remember or gather up from old books of the yearly Passover ritual, performing it devotedly and secretly, in danger of their lives.

A romanticized version of history in one of several partisan novels by Robert Hugh Benson, about the Catholics in England under Elizabeth I, has one scene that comes through with vivid reality. A girl brought up in the newly respectable reformed faith attends a secret Mass celebrated by a hunted priest in the attic of a house. In the cramped room are old countrymen and women and high-born land-owners, the keenly intelligent and enthusiastic with the obstinate and unthinking faithful. And the ritual, in scarcely articulated Latin, hurried and subdued, still conveys to the girl, seeing it for the first time, the sense of something vitally important going on—always going on. Here, though there may be priest and congregation, none is audience, all are actors, but actors in devoted rehearsal for a performance that may never take place.

In this kind of situation there is great intensity, the Gospel ideal of oneness seems to be realized, and subjectively, in the minds of some present, it probably is. But there is an element missing, just because this is a closed, predetermined group. It is not because the group is small that it lacks the essential element, but because, if only from necessity, the group has no power or intention of reaching beyond itself. There is no audience, the message resonates only within the group. No new echoes catch up the sound and send it back renewed. Rehearsals must go on, the play must not be forgotten, but it needs to be aware of future performances, at least in hope. Otherwise there is the danger that the rehearsal form will become permanent, and when the outside world is able to watch once more, all that will be seen is the same repetition, the preserved and surviving forms. These will have a strong significance, but it will be the significance of the history of a surviving devoted elite, not the significance of a transforming message of present hope for all those who are willing to hear and assist.

This is not the same situation as in religious traditions in which the enactment of sacred drama symbolizing historical and cosmic events is a regular and explicit part of life, for here the role of the audience, though definitely set outside the sacred area, is recognized and essential. The situation in the case of religious traditions that survive eras of persecution is more like that of exiled artistes, such as some troupes of refugee dancers from Eastern Europe who performed in England and America during and after the last war. For the troupers themselves, the work was a labor of love, preserving something of their own country and culture as well as possible. This was their motive and there was really little possibility of communication with the audience at this level. They attracted audiences, certainly, but these audiences came to wonder at the beauty of traditional dances whose very strangeness and incomprehensibility was the attraction. Such an art had grown up as essentially a common cultural experience in which dancers and spectators shared an understanding of the meaning of the dance, perhaps as an historic and patriotic re-presentation but also essentially as present celebration. There was a continual exchange between audience and dancers, and indeed such events, when they occurred in country towns and villages, were often part of a fair or festival and were followed by nonprofessional dancing and general jollification. To put such dancing on a stage in a foreign land, before an audience which, however appreciative, has no common cultural understanding, is not exactly to destroy it, but it is certainly to give to the audience an essentially passive and largely intellectual role.

This can be valuable, however. It can stimulate comparisons, study, curiosity about different ways of thinking and feeling. It can, indirectly, feed the desire for a truly transforming experience, and it can even create one. I have seen a London audience moved to tears and almost penitential fervor by a Polish dance troupe at a time when Poland was in the grip of the worst of the Nazi horror. But this is accidental and due to circumstances which are not inherent in the kind of relationship proper to such an audience and such a group of players. The distinction remains, and it is one that has caused much of the loss of contact between the old churches and the descendants of the regular churchgoers. For when a cultural tradition is broken, whether by war or social upheaval, the ancient and well-accepted relationship between church and people vanishes with it.

From then on, the old play loses its natural audience, and the players are left to repeat the performance chiefly among themselves. New audiences may come, some because bits of the old tradition linger, some because it is beautiful and satisfying even if belief is hazy. The biggest outcry against changing the Prayer Book forms of the Church of England came from intellectuals, nonbelievers or half-believers, who valued the beauty of the language and music, having long lost contact with the beliefs they expressed. Some continue to come because the people who keep the old routines going are also known as active and inspiring players through other "fringe" performances (not in the sense of less important but of "unofficial" productions played during the course of an "official" cultural festival) such as prayer meetings, social-work enterprises, or solo acts like healing and preaching. But the deep cultural unity has gone for good, and this is why tinkering with liturgical forms is only marginally effective, and hopes of renewal through liturgy have faded. A new relationship between actors and audience has to be sought. This means virtually remaking not only the play but all our ideas about drama, though its meaning doesn't change because it is about salvation, the reality of human life and its destiny. It isn't enough just to offer what the convinced know to be good. In what way is it good?

What Peter Brook* says about the theater, we can say about Christian faith. He is talking here of the efforts to take the theater to the people and make the best in culture available to all:

Behind all attempts to reach new audiences there is a secret patronage—"you too can come to the party"—and like all patronage it conceals a lie. The lie is the implication that the gift is worth receiving. Do we truly believe in its worth? In a sense, all forms of audience-wooing flirt dangerously with this same proposition—come and share in the good life which is good, because it has to be good, because it contains the best. This can never really change so long as culture or any art is simply an *appendage of living, separable from it, and, once separated, obviously unnecessary.* [My italics.] Such art then is only fought for by the artiste to whom, temperamentally, it is necessary, for it is his life. In the theatre we always return to the same point: it is not enough for writers and actors to experience this compulsive necessity, audiences must share it too. So in this sense it is not just a question of wooing an audience. It is an even harder matter of creating works that evoke in audiences an undeniable hunger and thirst.

It is, rather, a matter of creating an awareness that the feelings are those of hunger and thirst, and therefore can be satisfied by food and drink. You don't do that by liturgical formulae, by involving yourself in the needs of the poor and oppressed, by preaching, or by speaking in tongues, though

* Peter Brook, *The Empty Space.* McGibbon & Kee, London, England. 1968.

all these actions are part of the drama of salvation, gestures and words that can only acquire meaning from the meaning of the play as a whole. It won't do just to use our own imagination, not even one drawing on Scripture and Christian history, even in contemporary clothing.

As Brook says again:

We have lost all sense of ritual and ceremony—whether it be connected with Christmas, birthdays, or funerals—but the words remain with us and old impulses stir in the marrow. We feel we should have rituals, we should do something about getting them and we blame the artistes for not finding them for us. So the artiste attempts to find new rituals with only his imagination as his source: he imitates the outer forms of ceremonies, pagan or baroque, unfortunately adding his own trappings—the result is rarely convincing. And after the years and years of weaker and waterier imitations, we now find ourselves rejecting the very notion of a holy stage. It is not the fault of the holy that it has become a middle-class weapon to keep children good.

The director, here, is more acute in his diagnosis than most churchmen. But if imagination and enthusiasm cannot make the salvation drama a part of life rather than a decoration, an extra, what can?

What is needed is an awareness that from time to time God rewrites his play, using new language and thereby evoking new ranges of feeling and association. An anthropologist was asked recently in a radio interview what he felt the West could learn from the threatened but still intact culture of the Xingu Indian tribes in Brazil. He did not reply, as expected, that they had secrets of healing herbs, a beautiful simplicity of life, or interesting myths, but he startled the interviewer by saying that by learning their language he had found himself able to put into words things in himself that had previously been inarticulate stirrings, mute feelings and desires never sufficiently defined to be satisfied. This is a nasty shock for the heirs of a cultural tradition as rich and sophisticated as that of the English language. It could work the other way just as well, no doubt.

The point is that no culture (which means, in the last resort, no language) is exhaustive. None can express all that human nature knows and longs for. And cultural change means the pushing to the surface of inarticulate experiences in search of explicit forms. Religious forms—not just liturgical but moral and doctrinal—have always this purpose of expressing and acting out what remains at least partly unsayable. Symbols and ritual are a part of language—a part of all language—but more explicitly of cultic language. And this is what we have to recognize and submit to. God rewrites his play in new languages, but it depends on the actors whether they can learn the new text.

In order to become aware of God's rewriting of the text of his play (and it is he who rewrites it for each age; we simply have to listen, and not insist on the old edition) we who are convinced Christians have to be open to the kind of shakeup that makes audiences responsive. Meditation on the life of Christ, which has always been a part of Christian devotion, should have just this effect if it is real; but even more so, should the pursuit of contemplative prayer, which undermines all self-satisfaction and strips away pretenses and defenses. Some groups of actors nowadays subject themselves and each other to savage psychological maulings in the attempt to make themselves more open to reality, as vehicles of truth capturing the message of the spirit in man as it speaks now, not last year or five hundred years ago, or even yesterday, since what makes live audience-actor relationship is present and can never be recaptured or repeated. Still, the immediacy works with a given range of forms in a given cultural setting. There is a double need: first to discover God's new version of the play, and then to evoke the desire for it and satisfy it with all possible selflessness and skill.

The actors' search for the way through to a new and real form that can reach audiences, not by way of heightened imagination but by the stripping of old securities, is reminiscent of the methods (now much frowned on) by which novices in religious houses used to be deliberately humiliated in elaborate and rather macabre ways—such as being made to do obviously useless things, and publicly reprimanded for faults they had never committed. This could easily be an exercise in concealed sadism, but the proper intention of such techniques was to jerk the novice out of reliance on his intelligence, his talents, or even his virtues and general sense of being acceptable. He was forced from one position to another, until nothing was left him but naked faith and a residual obstinacy about the reality of his own religious vocation. If he survived this, he might discover the meaning of salvation and be able to live it and communicate it. He might turn out a good actor.

That this is not merely a medieval idiosyncrasy is shown not only by the rehearsal techniques of actors but in other arts. A recent television film about young sculptors showed the first day for sculpture students at a particular art school. They were ushered, unprepared, into a large bare room, and each given a large cube of white polystyrene foam wrapped in brown paper. They were forbidden to talk to each other, though they could ask the instructor for tools. They were given no instruction, no time limit, no help, but left there to work or not work, together or singly. Thus all the normal reference points which a student relies on were removed. In this spiritual limbo each one was entirely on his own, and all his weaknesses were exposed to his own gaze, before he might begin to discover his strengths. Whatever he did make would be, not necessarily expert, but at least real and revealing, though it might reveal only the paucity of personal aesthetic resources normally augmented by clear models and direction.

So with Christians. In order to become aware of the new version of the play we have to be violently removed from our reliable fixed points. This can feel like a betrayal of the past and even of those who are now so much in need of the play's message. It can seem like sitting on the stage in silence, while the audience waits for the play to begin. But maybe that silence is what is needed, for a while, in order to make them into the Gospel kind of audience, open to an experience that drags them in, in which passivity and detachment are impossible.

As a small step toward this, as well as to elucidate (though the word doesn't quite describe the strange effect) further the relationship of actors, audience, and language, we can get some help of a rather backhanded kind from Tom Stoppard's play, *Rosencrantz and Guildenstern are Dead.**

* Tom Stoppard, *Rosencrantz and Guildenstern are Dead.* Grove Press, New York. 1967; Faber & Faber Ltd.

This play is so funny that it is easy not to realize that it is as devastatingly direct and upsetting as any Beckett tour-de-force. It keeps on knocking into, treading on, or otherwise encountering all the sorest bits of the contemporary mind, apparently by accident but with horrid accuracy, and in such a way that by the time the pain registers and produces a response of anger or fear, the action has moved somewhere else and the reaction is left in mid air, feeling foolish, much as the two heroes are themselves made to feel foolish.

It would be impossible to pin down what the play is about, except to say vaguely that it is about the human predicament, and therefore about death, identity, role-playing, meaning and nonmeaning, and other portentous headings that no sooner rise to consciousness than they are batted on the head and collapse ignominiously. But for my purposes, here, one of the strands of significance (meaning would be too restricting a word) has to do with this matter of being jerked out of the expected and the secure into a half or scarcely understood context of action, in which one operates by someone else's plan, yet the action is never explained, nor even clearly seen. It is, therefore, about the relation between actors and audience—which is which and where is it, or he or them, if it is me—that is, whichever I am. (Reading Stoppard produces this kind of verbal reaction, which is one of the play's maddening virtues.)

The two young men, unimportant characters used in Shakespeare's *Hamlet* to power a small bit of rather creaking plot machinery, here become the center of attention. Not the center of action, however, because they never manage to get involved in that, or even quite to discover what it is. All they know is that they've been summoned, peremptorily and urgently, from their usual and predictable lives, by a messenger. The King wanted them; they went. They can't remember much before or since, but they are discovered tossing coins that always come up heads. This is unnerving and a sign of the shift from the known to the bewilderingly unpredictable. In typical Stoppard fashion, it is the very fact that it's *always* heads—*i.e.,* totally predictable—which demonstrates their uprootedness from the security of chance. As "Guil" says: "This [the gambler's certainty that he wouldn't bet on a certainty] made for a kind of harmony and a kind of confidence. It related the fortuitous and the ordained into a reassuring union which we recognized as nature."

In this state of uprootedness, they eventually find they are being used by Claudius to find out (as in Shakespeare) what is worrying Hamlet, or at least that is what Claudius tells them. But they never really get the hang of it because they are, in fact, off-stage of some play which every now and then enters theirs. They try to cooperate, do what is required, but they never discover how to, or even if it's possible. Every now and then they try to force a showdown and discover exactly what is going on, but they lose their nerve at the last moment because it's safer, really, not to be sure than to be sure that everything is unsure and senseless, or worse—"Because if we happened, just happened to discover, or even suspect, that our spontaneity was part of their order, we'd know that we were lost."

In and out of the action—or inaction, as it seems mostly and frighteningly to be—come a group of Players, the ones hired by Hamlet to enact before his stepfather the play showing how (as Hamlet thinks) Claudius murdered his

brother and stole his brother's wife. These players, in Stoppard's play, are a ragged and amoral collection, willing to
put on (for a consideration) any kind of show that is required. "Let your imagination run riot, they are beyond
surprise," says the leader of the troupe. And when Rosencrantz, half repulsed and half fascinated by the prospect of
a private sex show ("It will cost a little to watch, and a little
more if you get caught up in the action"), inquires shyly,
"What exactly do you *do?*" the Player replies with lines that
provide one of the keys to the symbolism of the play:

We keep to our usual stuff, more or less, only inside out. We do on
stage the things that are supposed to happen off, which is a kind
of integrity, if you look on every exit as being an entrance somewhere else.

But as if this wasn't sufficiently confusing, the relation between actors and audience is tossed around, turned inside
out, mocked, reverenced, and finally revealed as something
terrifyingly close to the heart of human existence. "I recognized you at once," says the Player to Ros and Guil, "as fellow artistes."

Ros: I thought we were gentlemen.
Player: For some of us it is performance, for others, patronage.
         They are two sides of the same coin.

—as indeed the two young men discover, or half discover,
later, when the Players present (on board the ship that is
taking Hamlet and the two of them to England) a play in
which two spies are to be killed, and the friends realize that

the player-spies are wearing coats identical with their own. But they themselves, as they discover, are betrayed to death by the letter they think betrays Hamlet to death. The shifts of identity between player and audience are exploited in various ways, always so as to undermine confidence in accepted categories of behavior and relationship, even relationship to time of day or geographical position, as in the hilarious and frightening passage where Guil tries to discover their compass direction by reference to the sun, and the position of the sun by the time of day, and the time of day by the position of the sun, but is really trying to find out the direction of the wind. ("Why don't you go and have a look?" "Pragmatism? Is that all you have to offer?" "You seem to have no conception of where we stand!" And the play on words is unnerving as well as funny.)

The reason they want to know the direction of the wind arises from Hamlet's classically cryptic remark: "I am but mad north-north west. When the wind is southerly I know a hawk from a handsaw." They don't know what he meant (nobody does), and yet their slender hope of making sense of their own role is to make some kind of sense of his so that they can relate to it. They try desperately to make an active role for themselves, pretending that it was *their* plan to bring the Player to divert Hamlet from his melancholy. The Player strips away this delusion. He has a permanent entrée at Court, he tells them.

He and his troupe are Players, therefore essential. And we realize at one point that what the Player says about being actors is true of the human apprehension of what is required in order to be meaningfully alive at all. This is when the Players arrive at Court angry and deeply resentful because Ros and Guil, after wanting them to play a wayside interlude for them, had left them suddenly without an audience. It happened because this was one of the moments when the compass describing the circumference of the Shakespeare *Hamlet* drew its arc through whatever play the young men had previously been involved in (but they can never remember quite what it was) and swept them up into *that* action—every exit being an entrance somewhere else—leaving the Players still, for a while, outside the Court circle.

This desertion, the Player furiously explains, attacks the very fundamentals of their being—and ours:

You don't understand the humiliation of it—to be tricked out of the single assumption which makes our existence viable—that somebody is *watching*. The plot was two corpses gone before we caught sight of ourselves, stripped naked in the middle of nowhere and pouring ourselves down a bottomless well. . . .

And later:

We're actors. . . . we pledged our identities, secure in the conventions of our trade, that someone would be watching. And then, gradually, no one was. We were caught, high and dry. It was not until the murderer's long soliloquy that we were able to look around; frozen as we were in profile, our eyes searched you out, first confidently, then hesitantly, then desperately, as each patch of turf, each log, every exposed corner in every direction proved uninhabited. . . . Even then, habit and a stubborn trust that our audience spied on us from behind the nearest bush, forced our bodies to blunder on long after they had emptied of meaning, until like runaway carts they dragged to a halt. No one came forward. No one shouted at us. The silence was unbreakable, it imposed itself upon us, it was obscene. . . .

The word "obscene" itself sums up what this is all about. We often regard as obscene when publicly done or spoken, actions and words which are quite acceptable in private. Here the obscenity lies in the fact that what was essentially intended to be public—to have an audience—is discovered to be private. The implication is that human acts and words—even the most intimate or secret—only become real, true, dignified, to those who act and say them *because they are really known as part of a play,* and a play has an audience. However secret, for instance, a diary may be kept, it is objectively something to be read *by others.* We *need* an audience and if we feel the lack of one we create one in our heads. To discover that there is no audience is to lose meaning and therefore existence. If there were no salvation drama there would be no salvation, because we can only know who we are (people) and what we are capable of (salvation) when we act it, or see it acted, which are "two sides of the same coin." And anyway, every exit is an entrance somewhere else, into another play where the audience is being watched by the actors, who need them for their own play.

The language of the play tells us what we are doing—not all of what we are doing but enough to make sense of it. If we demand total sense the play collapses, there is only criticism. So we are bound to feel, like Ros and Guil, frequently confused and doubtful. Which is our play? Are we really in it? *Is* there a play or just a series of unconnected incidents? Do our own actions contribute something to the development of the action, or are we puppets? And what's *under-neath?*

We just have to live with these questions, and by living with them some acquire answers—of a kind.

CHAPTER 5

The Denouement

"UNKNOTTING" or "disentangling" is quite a good way to describe the final liberation of the human spirit from its tangle of fears and misdirected desires. It has obvious analogies with the satisfying "unknotting" of a dramatic plot, making all clear and fulfilled. But this human event, acknowledged and admired in great saints or mystics even by those who do not share their beliefs, seems not only separable from but ludicrously inconsistent with the set of doctrines that come under the heading of eschatology. Nothing so easily rouses the mirth or contempt of the humanist as religious language about life after death, the end of the world, heaven and hell. An eschatological language made from allusions and symbols that are no longer meaningful to most people has made the whole subject of the "last things" an embarrassment to many Christians, to be thought of as little as possible, submerged in the flood of socially involved Christianity; or, if necessary, explained away as a first-century millenarian obsession to be understood metaphorically. Yet, reasonably, the "end" of human life, not only individually but racially is the most important subject one could conceive.

The fact is, nobody knows, or can know, what events or experiences are summed up in such a title as the Second Coming of Christ, or what is implied in words like Heaven and Hell and Purgatory, or other symbolic references to the state of the dead or the final destiny of the cosmos. We simply use time-honored, symbolic phrases to express convictions about certain ultimate realities, convictions which seem to spring from deep within the human spirit at all times and places. This is not the place to argue about whether all this is a fabrication of the human mind seeking comfort in the face of final meaninglessness. Those with a settled opinion of this kind are usually so armored in their resistance to any more searching ideas that discussion is useless, and books like this one are in any case meaningless to them. All the same, the virtually universal occurrence of doctrines and myths of some kind about life beyond death, and some kind of final cataclysm, is a fact; and the Christian tradition about these things is definite, even if necessarily expressed in images whose significance is dependent on the cultural setting.

There have been many ways of conceiving of immortality, and not all have borne any resemblance to the Chris-

tian one of a personal but totally transformed mode of existence transcending all the limitations of earthly human
existence, but still human, and—as human—yet sharing
the life of the eternal Self of God. Some of the earliest docu-
mented notions of human immortality, in Sumeria and ancient Greece, seem to have assumed that one could be
immortal only by renouncing humanity and becoming a
god—an option for exceptional people only and not always
a comfortable existence. In any case, it was one that cut off,
as effectively as death itself, the promoted hero from friends,
family, and the happiness possible to mortals. The idea of
immortality as survival in the lives and minds of one's descendants is a recurrent one in Hebrew literature, and this
is given a deeper significance when the life of the individual
continues not only in his descendants but in the mind of the
eternal Yahweh himself. The later Greek and Roman concept of a shadowy, underworld life after death for all except
heroes is also found in Norse mythology. Valhalla (like the
Elysian fields) is for the hero raised to godhead, not for ordinary people who must go to the dark kingdom of Hel, the
goddess of death.

Men have always wrestled with the thought of death, and
the struggles of heroes like Gilgamesh, Hercules, or the
quest of Orpheus, express the power of the desire to snatch
the secret of life from the dark gods of the underworld. The
myths of all ages and cultures, including the Christian one,
express the striving for the light, and the almost universal
pessimism about the result of that struggle. Men, on the
whole, don't want to be gods, but to be comfortably human
for an indefinite period, even when the divinized state is

recognized as superior. Only the heroes *want* to transcend human nature, let alone have a chance of achieving transcendence.

The paradoxical view presented by the existentialist movement, however, is that only the heroes—those who have the courage to recognize the inevitability and finality of their own death—are truly human. The ones who opt for ordinary contentment and not thinking about death are by that evasion less than fully human. But the contradiction is only semantic, for the existentialist idea of being fully human involves a kind of conversion, a reaching out into the unknown in heroic surrender to what is apprehended as a destruction. This heroic act is psychologically equivalent to the surrender made in faith, for faith is a leap into the unknown and dangerous, whose demands are, by definition, beyond human control. Therefore, the existentialist "conversion" makes heroes (*i.e.* superhumans or gods) of mortal men, and their condition is equivalent to that of the divinized heroes of Valhalla. The fact that the existentialist rejects the possibility of life beyond death does not alter this because the divinized hero occurs in a myth. And the point of myth is to express areas of human experience that are not directly communicable in any other form. Their equivalence to realities at a different metaphysical level is another matter altogether. They are not evidence for or against an actual human existence beyond (or "inside," "above," "after," etc.) physical death. They can express the existentialist "becoming" in the instant of truly facing the reality of death, and they can also express the Christian martyr's steadfastness, itself like that of Jesus who endured death with "joy set before him." For the myth, at this level, is an expression of the perennial conviction that men and women can transcend their normal limitations and, by an heroic act, attain to an experience of living which is radically and qualitatively different from the normal one.

A myth can do this but it cannot do more. It is not, of itself, a transforming agent. It expresses the nature and possibility of transformation, but it is not easy to see how the form of the myth could engage the human mind in the process of fulfilling what is symbolized. It is not just a matter of inspiring the desire to emulate, for a myth can do this. For a conversion to happen and make the myth symbol an experienced reality, there has to be a demand of which the person is conscious, something reaching into the hidden self and calling it forth. The nature of this demand, and its relation to the *real* self which is so elusive, is illuminated by the creative actor's search for authenticity, which always eludes him.

The ordinary, talented, and reliable actor wants to perfect a technique which will enable him to go through a long run giving a good and dependable performance. He doesn't aim for anything more, and his only fear is that his technique will let him down and he will be exposed in his basic ineptitude to the eyes of the audience. He fears the uncovering of reality, because there lurks an unacknowledged fear that his reality is probably not worth much, indeed perhaps it does not exist at all. This is very similar to the unacknowledged fears of the person who wants religion to be a reassurance and a prop, not in the sense of making life easy (it is very hard work to be a thoroughly practicing churchman) but in the sense that a conscientiously practiced religion will give to his life a shape and value which is sufficient and valid. He does not want (and would refuse to see any value in) the heart-searchings and doubts and hopes of the converted. In fact, the word and concept of conversion had, and frequently still has, associations of overenthusiasm, emotional self-indulgence, and religious extremism which leave the necessities of real life to the practical and sane people. So the "solid" Christian (or his equivalent in other faiths) faces his death, his "first night," with anxiety, but his anxiety is about whether he has sufficiently polished his religious observances to stand even a divine critic's eye.

The attitude of the really converted is totally different, and the difference is clarified in a very striking way in Peter Brook's description of the creative actor's approach to the long process of preparation for *his* first night:

. . . The really creative actor reaches a different and far worse terror on the first night. All through rehearsals he has been exploring aspects of a character which he senses always to be partial, to be less than the truth—so he is compelled, by the honesty of his search, endlessly to shed and start again. A creative actor will be most ready to discard the hardened shells of his work at the last rehearsal because here, with the first night approaching, a brilliant searchlight is cast on his creation, and he sees its pitiful inadequacy. The creative actor also longs to cling to all he's found, he too wants at all costs to avoid the trauma of appearing in front of the audience, naked and unprepared—still this is exactly what he must do. He must destroy and abandon his results, even if what he picks up seems almost the same . . . this is the only way that a part, instead of being built, can be born. The role that has been *built* is the same every night, except that it erodes. For the part that is born to be the same it must always be re-born, which makes it always different. Of course, particularly in a long run, the effort of daily re-creation becomes unbearable, and this is where the experienced creative artist is compelled to fall back on a second level called technique to carry him through.*

The parallel is exact. The preparation for a first night for such an actor is not self-training, leading up to a moment of testing, after which all will be well. This is the image of human spiritual life encouraged by the long centuries when Christianity had become (unnoticed) a culture, a cosmology, and a set of customs, and not necessarily a re-birth or a personal change at all. The elite of those whose faith caught fire and transformed them were recognizably different, and religious life (the phrase itself is significant of the separation) was the normal way of embodying that difference. But the committed believer, like the creative actor, searches all his life for the truth, the Kingdom of Heaven, the self within him which he can never know more than partially in mortal life, and which yet empowers and informs his thoughts and actions insofar as it has been set free to do so. And this must always be done afresh, the re-birth is a constantly new discovery of the self, which can never be a possession to be counted on but a force transcending the individual's control or understanding—his very essence yet greater than himself.

Like any other human being, the committed believer fears the revelation of his basic nakedness, which is ultimately the nakedness of dying; but for him death is not a single far-off date to be prepared for but a constant companion. The refusal to rely on achieved results means that he is always forced to begin again from nothing, and it is

* Peter Brook, *The Empty Space.* McGibbon & Kee, London, England. 1968.

this nothing—as it seems to him—that is the only ultimate reality, the self beyond maneuvering or morality, let alone religious observance. The approach of death may throw a "brilliant searchlight," but the awareness of inadequacy is there from the beginning. It is not compensated for by a sense of the true creative power at work in the depths; on the contrary, a sense of inadequacy is the condition of that power.

This is an important point, one which all those who have searched strongly for truth have emphasized, and it is clear that a mere intellectual grasp of the idea is useless. It seems that the denudation of death has to be somehow acted, so that it may finally become a reality. There is definitely a dramatic (in the proper sense) touch to the behavior of saints of all faiths in their attempts to rid themselves of what prevents the fullness of freedom. The very vow of poverty taken by some who are thrusting away from a routine interpretation of the Christian drama is both a bodily and a symbolic expression of this always renewed stripping of exterior supports. But this, like any other performance, can become an observance, a mere technique, useful and necessary for exhausted human nature to fall back on, but by no means a way of freedom by itself.

The careers of many spiritual men and women have begun by dramatic gestures of renunciation, and no doubt the young enthusiast easily believes that the physical denudation is once for all, and really frees. It does, to some extent, but, as Peter Brook says, "he must destroy and abandon his results"—even the result of comparative psychological freedom, because even that can become something relied on. The comfortable self-image of the emancipated and spiritual person, unhampered by worldly concerns, can easily become a protection from a greater denudation, or a buffer against the sufferings of others. And even total self-giving, as the world sees it, is in danger of degenerating into mere technique. The great ones have always been aware of this, and it accounts in part for the long tradition in all faiths of emphasis on detachment. This can be taken to what may seem to the outsider as ridiculous lengths. For instance, when a work of great value to suffering people is abandoned by its creator at the orders of a superior, for the sake of preserving its creator's humility.

The abuses of religious obedience, the sometimes petty ways it is used, should not make us blind to the real sense behind. Like the moment of accepting death in the existentialist salvation, this willingness to renounce even the best, to be constantly reduced to nothing, is the condition of transcendence. It is not enough to know in theory one's inadequacy; the death must be experienced through and through. The inner and most secret dying comes about through the outer and even public destruction of the ego. This is beautifully demonstrated in the *Fioretti* of St. Francis, in the story about his definition of perfect joy. This joy is the freedom and transcendence which he, above all men, seemed to know, and yet which he, above all men, knew to be always endangered by the least little bit of reliance on achievement, even the achievement of great works of mercy and spiritual power:

When as Saint Francis was going one day from Perugia to St. Mary of the Angels with Brother Leo in the Springtide, and the very bitter cold grievously tormented him, he called to Brother Leo that was going on before and said thus:

"Brother Leo, though the Brothers Minor throughout the world were great examples of sanctity and truly edifying, nevertheless write it down and take heed diligently that not therein is perfect joy."

And going on a little further, Saint Francis called a second time:

"O Brother Leo, albeit a Brother Minor should give sight to the blind, make straight the crooked, cast out devils, make the deaf to hear, the lame to walk, the dumb to speak, and (greater still) should raise them that have been dead a four days' space, write that not therein is perfect joy."

And going on a little he cried aloud:

"O Brother Leo, if the Brother Minor should know all tongues and all sciences and all the Scriptures, so that he could prophesy and reveal not only the things to come but also the secrets of consciences and souls, write that not therein is perfect joy."

So he continues, saying that not in all knowledge of human researches into natural things and powers, or in gifts of prayer, or in preaching so eloquently as to convert the world, is perfect joy to be found.

And this manner of speech continuing for a full two miles, Brother Leo with much marvel besought him saying:

"Father, I pray thee in the name of God that thou tell me wherein is perfect joy."

And Saint Francis thus made answer:

"When we come to St. Mary of the Angels, all soaked as we are with rain and numbed with cold and besmirched with mud and tormented with hunger, and knock at the door; and the porter comes in anger and says 'Who are ye?' and we say: 'We be two of your brethren,' and he says 'Ye be no true men, nay ye be two rogues that gad about deceiving the world and robbing the alms of the poor; get ye gone,' and thereat he shuts the door and makes us stand without in the snow and the rain, cold and a-hungered, till nightfall, if therewithal we patiently endure such wrong and such cruelty and such rebuffs without being disquieted and without murmuring against him, and with humbleness and charity bethink us that this porter knows us full well and that God makes him speak against us; O Brother Leo, write that therein is perfect joy."

Saint Francis goes on to describe how the porter, finding them still there, might try to drive them away and further insult and abuse and even beat them severely, and that if they suffer all this "patiently and with gladness . . . thinking on the pains of the blessed Christ, the which we ought to suffer for the love of him, O Brother Leo, write that here and herein is perfect joy." And he gives the reason:

Then hear the conclusion of the whole matter, Brother Leo: Above all the graces and gifts of the Holy Spirit, that Christ granted to his beloved, is to overcome oneself, and willingly for the love of Christ endure pains and insults and shame and want: inasmuch as in all other gifts of God we may not glory, since they are not ours but God's; whence saith the Apostle "What hast thou that thou hast not received of God? And if thou hast received it of him, wherefore boastest thou thyself as if thou hadst it of thyself? But in the cross of tribulation and affliction we may boast, since this is ours, and therefore, saith the Apostle, I would not that I should glory save in the cross of our Lord Jesus Christ."

That which feels hurt is purely the unessential part of human nature, the feelings and desires which have not found freedom from anxiety and fear and false ambition and symbolic securities. These are hurt by humiliation, failure, pain, and all deathly experiences, because they are our necessary but also death-imposing protection from truth. "Human kind cannot bear very much reality." So our attempts to ward off reality must, in the search for freedom, be thwarted by the acting out of their death. Such attachments must actually and visibly and openly be destroyed, and nothing must be allowed to prevent this destruction, not even the highest and holiest gifts and achievements.

This need for externally acted destruction of what impedes the liberation of the spirit seems odd and even shocking to some people. The spirit of man seems to them to be too secret and immaterial a thing to be affected by grossly physical actions. It is true that physical asceticism alone can be an aberration, not because what the body does is irrelevant, but because good acting must be whole—gesture, word, and spiritual impulse must be indivisible. If the mental attitude is one of fear and calculation and hate then the results cannot be liberating. This is the basic and all-important difference between the death of the martyr and of the suicide. There have been cases where people have killed themselves for a cause, so that their suicide was a form of martyrdom. The distinction is obvious and only reinforces my point.

The urge, not only of mystics and saints, but also of people like mountaineers and explorers, actually to *seek* hardship, often of extreme kinds, becomes understandable if we realize the need to perform bodily actions which symbolize the destruction of all that impedes the liberation of the spirit. The climber who stands on the peak finds more than a beautiful view; he has reached the denouement of a great symbolic drama, which is enacted in and through his whole personality. Through him it touches the minds of perhaps millions of people who feel suddenly the stirring in themselves of a possible freedom, a reality beyond their normal experience. And there is no doubt that the sheer pain and danger of the climb is an essential part of the experience. A mountain railway may take sightseers to peaks higher than this, but they will not find liberation there, but perhaps they may get a hint of its possibility, and even that is worth having.

The mystic, following the well-trodden path of abnegation, recognizes hardship as the proper form which enacts the liberation by which perfect joy is attained. The long process of achieving total physical control, as in Yoga, is not an athletic program but a means whereby the body may be taught to serve the way of total freedom, and it is partnered by equally stringent techniques of mental discipline for the same purpose. A whole prescribed sequence of combined mind and body patterns enacts the process of attaining freedom.

The Western monastic tradition developed its own patterns of word and gesture designed to free the spirit, and did so in a similar way by "acting" aspects of the process of salvation. The singing of psalms; the bows, prostrations, and processions; the shifting groups of people in solemn celebrations; the big arm movements; the embraces and handwashing of liturgical ritual; as well as the lesser rituals that accompany meals, meetings, and other daily routines, are dramatic enactments of aspects of the spirit's quest for salvation. Sorrow for sin, acceptance of death, aspiration toward freedom, respect for the spirit in others, obedience to the needs of community, confidence in the reality of the spirit—all these and others are enacted, and even unconsciously this drama of salvation has a saving effect provided the inner intention corresponds.

It is not necessary for Shakespearean actors to understand every nuance of Shakespearean allusion, let alone of Shakespearean criticism, in order to give a good, even a brilliant, performance. It is enough to have a good understanding, and that instinctive feel for the direction and atmosphere of a part and of its context. Intellectual understanding helps, and a lack of it is hardly likely to produce a sensible interpretation (though Keen's portrayals seem to have owed more to personal aura than to any great grasp of the Shakespearean mood). But it is true nevertheless that the degree of intellectual grasp required depends very much on the type of personality, and the same is true of the essentially dramatic behavior associated with the search for final freedom—for death as a denouement, in fact. Certain teachers may have a profound and detailed grasp of exactly *how* the symbolic act is linked to the spiritual fact, but those who follow their teaching need not necessarily have an equal imaginative and intellectual range and precision. All that is needed is that they obey, but with an obedience informed by the same aspiration, the same courage and love and creative determination as inspired the teacher.

St. Francis as a mystical teacher was unusual in the West (but not in the East) in that his teaching was often given in the form of allusive sayings, jokes, examples like the one quoted, or even more often simply in dramatic actions without any words. His feel for the right dramatic gesture was unerring, from the day when he stripped naked before the bishop's court and handed all his clothes back to his father, to the day he asked to be laid, equally naked, on the floor so

that he might die as he had lived—with and in nothing but
"perfect joy." The strange interaction of mind and body in
the interior salvation drama could not be better symbolized
and also exemplified than in the most famous of the incidents of that famous life, when the theme of it was imprinted on the body itself, as if the actor's role became so
perfectly coordinated with his portrayal that his own face
changed to fit it. This can happen, and that it does shows
why we need to understand the dramatic experience in
order to recover an understanding of the relation of soul
and body in the process of salvation. The attempt to create
a role changes the actor as well as the audience. Playing the
role of Christ was the single aim of Francis's life and the
source of his teaching, so much so that (indeed this is true of
most Christian saints) he never asked himself *why* the imitation of Christ should be the way of salvation. He just knew
it was, and for him it was pre-eminently the role of the
suffering Christ which was "the means of grace and the
hope of glory," the one way of liberation *from* all that
confines us, and *into* perfect joy.

The *Fioretti* express this very exactly, but my italics may
help to show the ways this account of the event brings out
the basic dramatic nature of what happened; the interaction of public and inward action, of spirit and body, role
and personality, man and God:

The day following, to wit, the day of the Most Holy Cross, St.
Francis, on the morn before daybreak, knelt down betimes in
prayer before the door of his cell, and *turning his face eastwards,*
prayed in this wise: "O my Lord Jesus Christ, two graces do I
pray thee to grant unto me ere I die: the first, that while I live I

may *feel in my body and in my soul,* as far as possible, that sorrow, sweet Lord, that thou didst suffer in the hour of thy bitterest Passion; the second is, that I may *feel in my heart,* so far as may be possible, that exceeding love wherewith, O Son of God, thou wast enkindled to endure willingly *for us sinners* agony so great." And remaining a long time thus praying, he knew that God would hear him, and that, so far as might be possible to a mere creature, thus far would it be vouchsafed to him to suffer the aforesaid things. St. Francis, having this promise, began to contemplate most devoutly the Passion of Christ and his infinite love, and *the fervour of devotion waxed so within him that through love and through compassion he was wholly changed into Jesus.*

This is followed by the famous vision of the six-winged seraph which "had the form of a man crucified," a contradiction of immortal spirit and mortal—indeed dying—flesh which symbolized the very essence of the dramatic denouement of the spirit: the destruction of the flesh (in the Pauline sense) in order to set free the living spirit. In what follows we see the vision affecting not only Francis but all the country around, symbolically illuminating the darkness of a worldly and anxiety-ridden Church. Some of the phrases, indeed, recall that wild, untamed but essential raw material of the dramatic experience now channeled and strengthened to enormous power:

And being in this wonderment, it was revealed by the Seraph who appeared to him, that the vision *had been shown him in such form,* by divine providence, *in order that he might understand he was to be changed* into the express similitude of the crucified Christ in this wondrous vision, not by bodily martyrdom but by *spiritual fire.* Then the whole Mount of La Verna seemed to flame forth in daz-

zling splendour, that shone and illumined all the valleys round
about, as it were the sun shining on the earth. Wherefore the
shepherds that were watching in that country saw the mountain
aflame . . .

During this vision it is said Christ revealed to Francis certain things which at the time he could not express. The author of the *Fioretti* asserts that he did reveal them "after his
death," and, however this may be, the interpretation of the
vision attributed to Christ does express very well the power
of the fully liberated (saved) spirit, which has played out its
role and achieved its denouement, so that this peak experience is now able to draw others toward the peak, like the
fame of a great climber. The "souls in prison" visited by
Christ after his death, in that mysterious article of the
Creed beloved of medieval artists, are equated with the
souls imprisoned by sin, the unliberated, whether one thinks
of this condition of Purgatory as an after-death cleansing or
a leading-up-to-death process of painful disentanglement.
And Francis, now completely in the role of Christ the Saviour—that is, fully liberated—can, like Christ, save others
from prison:

"Knowest thou," said Christ, "what I have done to thee? I have
given thee the stigmas that are the mark of my Passion, in order
that thou be my standard bearer. And even as I, on the day of my
death, descended into limbo and delivered all the souls I found
there by virtue of these my stigmas, so do I grant thee that every
year, on the day of thy death, thou mayst go to purgatory and de-
liver all the souls thou shall find there of thy three orders—Mi-
nors, Sisters, and Penitents—and others likewise that have a great
devotion to thee, and *thou shalt lead them up* to the glory of paradise

in order that thou be *conformed to me in thy death, even as thou art in thy life.*" This wondrous vision having vanished, after a great space, this secret converse left in the heart of St. Francis a burning flame of divine love, exceeding great, and in his flesh, a marvellous image and imprint of the Passion of Christ. For the marks of the nails began anon to be seen on the hands and feet of St. Francis, in the same manner as he had seen them on the body of Jesus Christ crucified that had appeared to him in the form of a seraph: and thus his hands and feet seemed nailed through the middle with nails. In like fashion, the image of a lance-wound, unhealed, inflamed and bleeding was seen on his right side. . . .

Wherefore his companions, before they learned these things from him, perceiving nevertheless that he never uncovered his hands or his feet, and that he could not put the soles of his feet to the ground, and finding thereafter that his tunic and nether garments were all bloody when they washed them, knew of a surety that he had the image and similitude of our Lord Jesus Christ crucified, expressly imprinted on his hands and feet, and likewise on his side.

The phenomenon of stigmata rouses furious controversy, since marks similar to those of Francis can occur in some kinds of mental illness involving delusions. This is an example of the same thing remarked earlier—that a creative portrayal of a role has to be properly integrated at every level. Certain outward gestures that belong to integrated performance can be imitated by anyone who cares to do so, but they are not acting, they are merely a stunt, or an eccentricity of a more or less extraordinary kind. What matters here are not the stigmata, which may be manifestations proper to one kind of temperament rather than another, but the intensity of the dramatic denouement, after the pattern of the denouement of Calvary—but symbolically, not literally. Just as the actual historical death of Jesus was *both* an inevitable political execution *and* the climax of salvation drama, not accidentally combined but essentially united, so the representation of that passion in Francis was *both* the result of a combination of temperament and culture *and* a re-presentation, effective in the same way at its own level, of the denouement in the salvation drama of Christ's sacrifice.

This denouement, then, is essentially a death, even when it goes on partly within the term of earthly life. It is about death because the raw material of the spirit is so entangled with a bodily experience distorted by countless generations of ignorantly directed and undirected desires, fears, and passions that only the radical disentanglement of death can set free the spirit. The Christian notion is that, once disentangled, the spirit can once more inform the liberated wholeness of human nature, though imagination cannot grasp the meaning of that and it can only be expressed in such concepts as the resurrection of the body and the everlasting life of Heaven. Once disentangled (and at any point *to the extent of its disentanglement*) the spirit has the saving power of the Saviour, and is involved on the "inside" in the salvation drama, strongly stirring the forces of participation which draw people into the center of action.

The existentialist insight, that it is only in the acceptance of death that man reaches full humanity, is verified; but it goes further because that acceptance has the transcendent quality of the heroic act, which removes men and women from the everyday-ness of unliberated humanity. It rejects the homely ambitions and seems to ordinary men and women heartless and inhuman in just the same way that the aspiration to godhead seemed undesirable to the world of Homer. (Odysseus struggled not toward transcendence but for secure domesticity!) The paradox that the heroic abnegation might be acted out in circumstances of uneventful and homely relationships was a comparatively late discovery. Even though it is written into the Gospels quite explicitly, the tradition that heroism is for the exceptional—not just in character but in circumstances—died hard and indeed lingers still. This is the reason why most of us continue from generation to generation tied to the 'wheel of things,' and with no particular desire to get off it.

The denouement of the drama of salvation is, however, not merely an individual one. It is not even a matter of one individual, like Francis, helping to free others by the power of his wholly available spiritual being. The myths of many nations and ages, and the traditional doctrines of Christianity, indicate a denouement on a cosmic scale, bringing the world as we know it to an end and replacing it by a new and transformed life. In the Greek view this would be merely the beginning of another cycle doomed to repeat itself indefinitely. The Buddhist sees the cycle as the result of desire—that is, misdirected desire, since the desire for enlightenment and freedom is the only true object—which ties mankind to material things, so that freedom means total disentanglement from sensible experience, relationship, and even individual existence. These things are *illusion*, they do not belong to the ultimate reality, the self. The denouement is, therefore, a dissolution of creation rather than a transformation, though the difference can sometimes seem to be one of philosophical structure rather than of spiritual experience. The experience of the enlightened and liberated self sums up all possible excellence and, therefore, in a sense is the fulfillment of the person as the Christian tradition sees it.

The Christian myths definitely refer to "a new heaven and a new earth," when the old have passed away. Like human beings themselves, the cosmos will be changed and reborn through death. Indeed the older tradition does not see individual liberation except in the person's involvement in the cosmic renewal.

The scope of this book is limited by the particular tool which is here used to explore the nature of salvation. The dramatic experience can provide a clue to the nature of this communal and cosmic, as well as individual, transformation scene, but it cannot be a substitute for myth or cosmology. I have used many different aspects of the dramatic experience to provide a way in, through recognizable doors, to a region of experience of which only the outer areas can be described or recorded, and even then only in open-ended images or in myths. At the point we have reached, that of attempting to provide a toe hold in this final region, we are talking about something which is beyond any kind of individual experience.

The mythologies of final cataclysm, and the cosmologies adjusted to fit them, in whatever culture, do not have obvious links with identifiable human experience. As we saw at the beginning of the chapter, this theme of final and cosmic denouement is universal, yet of all religious themes, even to the sincerely pious, it is the least credible, the most easily set aside in the realm of the peripherally important. Only occasional saints and mystics take it seriously, in visions of destruction and doom and glory which are formed in the myth-imagery of their own time and culture. Often, too, such visions do not seem to be clearly related to a final apocalyptic crisis, but turn out, in the visions of Purgatory of St. Catherine of Genoa, for instance, to have a much clearer reference to experiences of normal spiritual growth. In the case of St. Catherine, the visions seem to describe very exactly the meaning and effect of sin as people know it, are shut in by it, and suffer intensely in this realization. But the suffering itself is the necessary means of liberation. Whatever the interpretation put upon such visions by the seers themselves, they really tell us nothing about the cosmic denouement, but only (possibly) about the personal one, and about the role of the Saviour's passion in bringing it about, as we saw in the case of St. Francis.

Yet there seems to be a sense in which the personal denouement and the decisions it requires are the triggers of the cosmic resolution. Or is it the other way round? Is it the refusal to take the decision involving one in the total drama of salvation that means human failure, damnation? At the end of *Rosencrantz and Guildenstern are Dead*, when Ros has already disappeared (since the action of the "play" no longer requires him), Guil does not notice this but continues to speculate on the meaning of it all, and why they are thus left in the debris of drama with nothing to do, no motives, no role to play at someone's order, however senseless. And he wonders how it all began, whether they could have avoided this senseless "absence of presence" which is, as he knows, what death is—absolute death, "a gap you can't see, and when the wind blows through it, it makes no sound." That is death as damnation, total senselessness, "the second death" that the myths evoke with all the power of the great images of destruction.

But destruction *destroys*, makes naught. It negates the urge to know, to be, to have meaning. Is it inevitable, like the realm of the goddess Hel, the dim and meaningless underworld of Greek mythology, or the "grave" of Hebrew literature, which reduces man to a futility only mitigated by the memories of the living? The play suggests (perhaps "suggests" is too strong a word—it barely lets drift past a frail dried leaf of possibility) that there *was* a choice. One didn't *have* to be moved around amorally, mindlessly, by other people's distorted passions, strong as they are—". . . the carnal, bloody and unnatural acts/Of accidental judgments, casual slaughters,/Of deaths put on by cunning or forced cause/And, in the upshot, purposes mistook,/Fall on the inventor's heads. . . ."

All the self-justifying, elaborate, interlocking, and convincing apparatus of sin *can* be refused:

Guil: Our names shouted in a certain dawn . . . a message . . . a summons. . . . There must have been a moment, at the beginning, where we could have said—no. But somehow we missed it.

So he goes out as the spotlight on him goes out, and the main stage lights go up to reveal the corpses and mourners of the final scene of *Hamlet*, a potent symbol of the intricate mess human beings make when they isolate means and ends. The fascination of the play is partly in the tension it creates in the audience, because Ros and Guil *need not* be involved to their destruction in the mindless cruelties and selfishness of Shakespeare's cast—themselves only creations of another's brain, as we know all the time. In one way Ros and Guil are at two removes from reality, and in another they *are* the reality. They are voices in ourselves, not asking but provoking questions about death, judgment, hell, and responsibility. When the spotlight goes out on each in turn, it means (at one level at least) that dramatic denouement in the usual sense is unreal, contrived to satisfy the cowardice that cannot face "the endless time of never coming back." Shakespeare's Hamlet himself, after all his earlier self-torturing speculations about the nature of death, has nothing to say about it when he actually dies. His last words are about those who will live on after him: "The rest is silence."

It is silence because the final revelation and unwinding of the human drama goes beyond words. The well-made play is a satisfying entertainment, but the play that jerks an audience into life, that makes people wish they could tear their eyes away, yet know they will never be quite the same again—this kind of drama is not neatly rounded but leaves a gap, an unsaid knowledge, a dark hole of reality too real to be subjected to dramatic construction. In Shakespearean tragedy this gap is often the one between potentiality and fulfillment—the might-have-been hero who is corrupted, yet we never lose sight of what he might have been, like Macbeth, or Othello, or Richard II. Greek tragedy makes a gap yawn between the flexible growth of the human spirit and the arbitrary fate that rules it unseeing. It is not on either side of the gap that dramatic truth is to be found, but in the pit itself.

When the Clown brings Cleopatra the asp in the fig basket, his foolish tactlessness, his malapropisms and kindly, misplaced warnings about the unreliable nature of "wormes" bring together the homely earthiness of everyday, necessary living, and the experience of high tragedy at its culminating point. Unhindered, Cleopatra's suicide would be a perfect romantic apotheosis. The clumsy countryman is insensitive to the tragedy, doesn't know when to stop talking, but keeps on coming back to repeat his superfluous but well-meant cautions. The tension of this encounter brings the scene to a gut-clawing pitch of intensity before letting the tragedy take its course to a foreseen conclusion. Yet it is not Cleopatra's actual death that is the moment of truth, but that unspeakable gap which opens between two kinds of experience which are incompatible.

It is this gap, this silence, that destroys certainties and undermines reason. It brings the structures of man's mind toppling—and his greatest artistic triumph is to make that destructive experience available, within limits which are bearable. This is also the function of religious ritual and doctrine—to frame the approach to the ultimate experience, which annihilates all experience, in such a way that human beings can come to it without being destroyed or frightened away. Like some kinds of theatrical productions, religious ritual can, rather, protect people from awareness of the gap, but the supporting and encouraging process is not the less necessary because it has been misused (or rather its proper use has been semi-deliberately overlooked), often with the best of intentions.

So the dramatic experience illumines, or rather darkens, our understanding of the cosmic denouement by its ability to "frame" the finally incommunicable. It does this in various ways according to the form proper to that type of drama. Significantly, proper religious drama such as the medieval miracle plays or the modern Bible plays seldom does this because the symbolism is on a single level, using a sacred narrative "straight," without relating it to everyday experience, since the two are assumed to be identical. This is the special charm of medieval religious drama, but it was also the weakness of the medieval world view, which ended by making so complete a cosmology that there were no creative gaps left and people like mystics who fell into gaps were regarded with considerable suspicion by the official Church.

The ritual drama of the Passover, however, built up over centuries in the semi-accidental way in which ritual normally develops, lacks this conscious one-level symbolic form. Its symbolism is only partly intentional, or rather—like that of the Christian Eucharist—symbolic value became attached in the course of time to some acts which were originally purely practical, or whose meaning had been forgotten. But the fact that such obscure acts survive and are repeated and acquire symbolic value is a measure of their unconscious importance and significance. They are often the edge of that gap in which the encounter with the sacred, above all, takes place.

There is one moment in the Seder ceremony—as the recalling of God's mercies and their re-enactment, the rejoicing in being his people, the blessing and drinking of wine, the eating and thanksgiving, are almost over—when what is left to be done is a sort of happy anticlimax of singing and family jollification. At this point, when the tense and structured drama is beginning to run down, and only the fourth cup remains to be drunk, there is an odd little ceremony which seems to have nothing to do with the rest. After the third cup has been drunk with the invocation "to Peace," the cups are refilled, including an extra one, and the door is then opened, to let in Elijah. But instead of a suitable prayer for the coming of the traditional precursor of the longed-for Messiah, what follows is some verses of denunciation of the heathen, and prayer for their destruction. It is strangely out of keeping with the happy, united atmosphere of the rest, and some have suggested that these verses reflect centuries of horrific persecution of Jews, which they could not forget especially at Passover, for this was the time of year when persecution often broke out. This may be so, but whatever the historical reason may be, there is something else going on which cannot be thus explained. The suddenly opened door, the welcome offered to a guest who does not come, the anachronistic words of anger and revenge, all create a dramatic "gap," a "moment of truth," in which something is glimpsed through the open door, something more awe-ful, more beautiful, more intense, than the wonder and joy of the rest of the ritual. The ritual is completed and yet contradicted by this odd moment.

The phase of the "naturalistic" theater of the last fifty years, although it produced a large crop of unmemorable comedies and trite tragedies, made possible the intensely dramatic use of actual silence in order to create this "gap," this essential, shattering encounter with the truth that cannot be expressed. Pinter is a master of silence, and in *Old Times*, for instance, the entire dialogue is punctuated by long silences and short pauses, during which nothing happens at all. What happens is *Nothing*, equivalent to the mystic's *Nothing* which is also *All;* because in these silences the underlying truth about the relationships, which none of the three characters ever utters, makes itself felt. This Nothing is bigger than the content of the dialogue, much bigger than the little group on the stage, or even than the combination of audience and cast. In the same way in *The Caretaker*, although the pauses are not so much a part of the structure of the dialogue, there is an awareness all through that the reality of the situation between the three men is what is *not* being said. It would not be too much to say that Hell is what can be glimpsed in the space between the characters and their words. The two brothers torment the stupid, dishonest, self-deceiving Davies; they cheat him and cheat each other and themselves, and nobody says anything true, yet terrifying moral judgments are demanded of the audience by those gaps in statement. In Beckett's *Waiting for Godot*, the never-described person they are waiting for, who never comes, is not just a comment on the futility of human hope. He is by far the most powerful element in the play, indeed he makes the play. He is a looming, impossible, dangerous Nothing, around whom human beings scurry on their meaningless concerns, keeping busy and making jokes and just talking to hide the gap, and occasionally seeing it, but never for long, because "human kind cannot bear very much reality."

But when the gap is entered, the darkness accepted, then the real denouement happens.

Hence I observed how needful it was for me to enter into the darkness, and to admit the coincidence of opposites, beyond all the grasp of reason, and there to seek the truth where impossibility meeteth me. . . . For Thou hast shown me that Thou canst not be seen elsewhere than where impossibility meeteth and faceth me. Thou hast inspired me, Lord, who art the Food of the strong, to do violence to myself, because impossibility coincideth with necessity, and I have found that the place wherein Thou art unveiled is girt round with the coincidence of contradictions, and this is the wall of Paradise wherein Thou dost abide.

This is the analysis of Nicholas of Cusa, an intellectual, wrestling with what defeats the intellect. Catherine of Genoa, more vivid in language, says the same thing:

I see without sight, I understand without intelligence, I feel without feeling, I taste without taste, I know neither shape nor dimension, yet without seeing I see so divine a preparation that all words concerning perfection, cleanness or purity which I uttered before now seem to me naught but mockery and fable in comparison with this truth and honesty.

We can see here that the darkness, which is Hell and destruction to the cowardly and cruel and dishonest, is the pinnacle of bliss to the one who has allowed dishonesty to be burned away by the terror of truth. The dramatic use of effective silence is not just a trick to heighten tension, but a fundamental, if unconscious, statement of the nature of reality. It is in the gaps that the quality of the human situation is revealed.

The gap is not always indicated by actual silence, and in Shakespeare the accepted dramatic forms did not use silence as a part of the text, but the underlying creative darkness is just as powerfully apparent. In *King Lear* the babbling, helpless old man who can't make any sense of his surroundings represents as near an approach to that ultimate and frightening human truth as can be imagined. He has shed the arrogant blindness of his earlier power, and also the impotent rage of his first downfall. What is left is, in a sense, nothing humanly desirable. Lear is a "man of sorrows" and, like Jesus flogged and crucified, he evokes revulsion, or contempt, or pity. (Isaiah's "suffering servant" is the archetype of humanity degraded to a point where it challenges conversion or rejection—because no ordinary responses are available to cope with such a confrontation.) Only Cordelia, the completely truthful and even paradisiacally innocent ("Thou has a Daughter who redeems Nature from the general curse which twaine have brought her to."), is able to respond fully to this Nothing. Properly, her reconciliation with a father thus made into a dramatic Nothing, leads immediately to her death. "Thou art a Soule in blisse," says the mad king, and symbolically she is so, already. Her two sisters die, too, by murder and suicide, as a result of that same contact. Their natures are evil, so their contact with the dangerous challenge of the old king's witlessness condemns them, just as surely as it saves Cordelia, by revealing their hellish—and her heavenly—nature.

Lear, like Jesus, is a "stone of stumbling," he provokes final truth, for good or ill. It is fitting that it is Lear himself —at this point the embodiment of the "impossibility" of Nicholas of Cusa, the "unknowing" and "darkness" of all the mystics—who is the one who avenges Cordelia. Indeed, all the characters are revealed and condemned, or reconciled, according to their reaction to this central point of non-sense, the witless, dying King who is thereby also Saviour; and the audience is, as always, involved in this judgment. As the parallel with the archetypal Passion shows, the implications are much wider than mere judgment on the spiritual condition of these particular people. The audience is confronted by a darkness whose dimensions are universal and eternal. It is the Day of Judgment, and it is the sacrificed lamb who judges, not in apocalyptic symbol but in psychological reality. This moment embraces *both* the particular and the general, which is what gives it its power.

It is, as usual, T. S. Eliot (in "East Coker")* who comes nearest to expressing in words the exact way in which the general touches the particular, the eternal meets time, in human experience. He uses here a theatrical image. It is only accidentally dramatic, yet perhaps the more important for that, because the unsettling and emotion-heightening effect of scene-change in a conventional theater was never intended to be part of the dramatic build-up, yet certainly becomes so in many people's experience:

I said to my soul, be still, and let the dark come upon you
Which shall be the darkness of God. As, in a theatre,
The lights are extinguished for the scene to be changed
With a hollow rumble of wings, with a movement
     of darkness on darkness,
And we know that the hills and the trees, the distant panorama
And the bold imposing facade are all being rolled away—
Or as, when an underground train, in the tube, stops too
     long between stations
And the conversation rises and slowly fades into silence
And you see behind every face the mental emptiness deepen
Leaving only the growing terror of nothing to think about;

* From "East Coker" in *Four Quartets* by T. S. Eliot, copyright, 1943, by T. S. Eliot; copyright, 1971, by Esme Valerie Eliot. Reprinted by permission of Harcourt Brace Jovanovich, Inc., Faber & Faber Ltd.

Or when, under ether, the mind is conscious but
    conscious of nothing—
I said to my soul, be still, and wait without hope
For hope would be hope for the wrong thing; wait
    without love
For love would be love of the wrong thing; there is
    yet faith
But the faith and the love and the hope are all in the waiting.

Waiting for what? The whole point is that such a question is unanswerable in any terms that make sense to our time-and-sense limited minds. The extravagant imagery of apocalyptic literature makes one thing clear, and that is the completeness of the required destruction of all that we normally cling to, if the true self, not just of the individual but of all creation, is to be set free. St. Francis recognized the necessary process for the discovery of perfect joy, and the same conditions apply to the transformation of the cosmos, for man is unique, and yet unique only as the essential part of a total development. His proper development depends on the proper development of all life, and nonhuman life requires his dependent yet uniquely powerful cooperation.

St. Paul was not a man sensitive to natural things. He only mentions them as illustrations, often rather strained, of points to do with human salvation. Yet he clearly took it for granted that all creation, *including* man, was permeated with the same spirit and bound up together in the process of salvation. There is no suggestion in the famous passage in Romans (quoted below) that the notion was new or unfamiliar to his readers. The essential unity of creation is a premise of his argument, not a conclusion. The thought here illumi-

nates the line of Eliot's thinking and draws together much
of the struggling speech of the mystics from whom, indeed,
Eliot derived the concepts expressed in the passage from
"East Coker." The parenthetical comments in the following
quotation from Paul are in the interest of clarity.

I consider that the sufferings of this present time are not worth
comparing with the glory that is to be revealed to us. (The
"glory" is clearly not just individual salvation but something
much bigger, the "glory" of biblical theophanies.) For the creation waits with eager longing for the revealing of the Sons of God
(Man's crucial and yet integral role in cosmic salvation is quite
clear here.); for the creation was subjected to futility (meaninglessness, impotence, the frustration of its powers and capabilities),
not of its own will (nonhuman life does not make *decisions*) but by
the will of him who subjected it in hope (creation, by its inevitable
involvement in man's sin—that is its subjection to man's actual
and potential misunderstanding and misuse—is involved also in
the hope of salvation, as it could not otherwise have been); because the creation itself will be set free from its bondage to decay
and obtain the glorious liberty of the children of God. (The implication, once more, is that the rest of creation finds its own liberty
only by its involvement in man's salvation; yet the next bit shows
creation as *itself* desirous and yearning toward salvation. The two
ideas have to be kept together.) We know that the whole creation
has been groaning in travail together until now, and not only the
creation, but we ourselves, who have the first fruits of the Spirit,
groan inwardly as we wait for adoption as sons, the redemption of
our bodies. For in this hope we were saved. Now hope that is seen
is not hope. For who hopes for what he sees? But if we hope for
what we do not see, we wait for it with patience (Romans 8:18–
25).

The image of childbirth is interesting here, for it brings together two aspects of the denouement idea which are impossible to reconcile. One is the "outside time and space" element implied in the idea of the gaps in the drama, the truth that is unspeakable and can only be "framed" by dramatic action and words. The other is the historical element, the idea of a conscious and organic process unfolding to a proper conclusion, an identifiable dramatic finale. These two elements do not integrate. One, indeed, is nearer to the Eastern religious tradition which sees reality as wholly transcending the material world of time and sensation. The material world is illusion, not in the usual sense of existing only in the mind of the deluded person but in the sense of being irrelevant to the ultimately discovered and liberated self, which transcends and discards that world.

But the historical process of salvation is a Judaeo-Christian concept in which God is involved in history, works through it, and is everywhere immanent, but is also independently apparent in the events of human life, making them significant for salvation. Paul's image, however, brings the two together for the process of childbirth in creation has a definite sequence. It moves towards an expected moment which is that of birth; therefore, the acts and feelings of labor have a definite significance in relation to the outcome, they are not "illusion." Yet that which is to be born, the spirit, the self of the whole creation, the total Christ, is not definable or explainable in terms of that process. It is transcendent and "different." It is the darkness, the "gap" where dramatic development gives way to its end, which is unknowable and "mad" as old Lear.

This process of giving birth to the finally inexpressible is the dramatic process, and the drama of salvation is discovered to follow this pattern in the human soul, and in the whole cosmic development as seen by mystics and in the insights of religious teachers. The emphasis varies so much that the whole balance of feeling and attitudes to daily life can seem to have nothing in common, but the two elements (of significant development giving way to the totally *other*) are present in some form. Even the Buddhist mystic depends on the teaching and symbols of the Way, handed down for generations, and also on relationships as the teacher imparts it to the disciples. He believes that good actions lead toward liberation, while the Christian activist (as long as he is Christian and not just active) sees the *other* cutting across, and also underlying, purely political and practical decisions, and giving them saving significance as well as ethical punch.

The dramatic experience shows that the myths of life, death, and eternity can only be saving statements when they are dramatized. That is, they must be experienced as a process of significant human development in which people are involved both communally and at the deepest personal level. Such myths must satisfactorily engage reason, imagination, and bodily feeling (again both communally and personally) and lead to a denouement whose necessity is inescapable but whose nature is inapprehensible in the terms of the dramatic form. The experimental theaters of recent decades have all been trying to recover the power of that inexpressible underlying reality, which routinely entertaining drama had successfully obliterated, much as the socially acceptable forms of religious behavior had done. The raw material of salvation needs to be discovered, but as long as it is merely raw it has no significance. It requires dramatic form, and that form is the "play" of salvation—in the individual, in salvation history, and in the cosmic unfolding of existence itself.

The power of the spirit is in both the dramatic forms and in the gap they uncover. Salvation is not separated from ordinary life, it is its meaning. It is a dramatic yet a homely salvation.

Odysseus' search for domestic happiness turns out to have the same raw material as the passion of Francis for the Cross or of Nicholas of Cusa for the divine contradiction.

In the words of the tenth-century Eastern mystic, Symeon the Younger:

I saw him in my home. Among all those everyday things he appeared unexpectedly and became unutterably united and merged with me, and leaped over to me without anything in between . . . and I, who was in the midst of all things, am outside of them. . . . And now, verily, I am in that place where there is only light, and where the light is simple, and in beholding it, I emerge in simplicity and innocence.